Before We Say I Do
7 Steps to a Healthy Marriage

Marvin A. McMickle

Judson Press
Valley Forge

Before We Say I Do: 7 Steps to a Healthy Marriage
© 2003 by Judson Press, Valley Forge, PA 19482-0851
All rights reserved.

Scripture taken from the HOLY BIBLE, NEW INTERNATIONAL VERSION. Copyright © 1973, 1978, 1984 International Bible Society. Used by permission of Zondervan Publishers.

Library of Congress Cataloging-in-Publication Data

McMickle, Marvin Andrew.
    Before we say I do: 7 steps to a healthy marriage / Marvin A. McMickle
    p. cm.
    Includes bibliographical references.
    ISBN 0-8170-1443-8 (alk. paper)
        1. Marriage—Religious Aspects—Christianity. I. Title
BV835.M347 2003
248.8'44—dc21   2003045804

Printed in the U.S.A.
10 09 08 07 06 05 04
10 9 8 7 6 5 4 3 2

Before We Say I Do

Contents

Foreword

AMONG THE MOST DISTURBING cultural trends in recent decades has been the dissolution of marriages at an alarming rate. We have heard many times the statistic that some fifty percent of marriages end in divorce. When divorce occurs, it is more than just two people who are affected. Divorce hurts children, families, and even communities.

Aside from the issue of divorce is the question of unhappy and unfulfilling marriages. While I highly respect and support the commitment of two people to stay together regardless (so as to fulfill their vows to one another), I am saddened to encounter any marriage that is not as happy and strong as it should and could be.

Strong marriages form the basis of strong families and healthy societies; they enable people to live more contented and productive lives. Therefore, it is incumbent on churches, and especially pastors, to do all we can to enable people to establish strong, healthy marriages. We must provide people, especially young people, with the right perspective that is required for making wise decisions concerning marriage. We must provide the tools that will help them to build and, when necessary, to do repair work.

I have found in my experience as a pastor that a weak marriage is one where extensive counseling should have occurred before taking those important steps to the altar. When two people testify that they are in love, it can be awkward and difficult to raise questions about how successful their marriage will be after the intense emotions fade, as they inevitably will. But I believe that these young persons, whether they know it or not, are depending on their pastors and parents to raise these difficult questions and thus to protect them against future disappointment and confusion.

Detailed, scholarly, research-based marriage manuals have their place, but they cannot take the place of the compassionate wisdom that springs from Rev. Dr. McMickle's experience of counseling engaged and married couples in a Christian context. This wisdom, gleaned from over two decades of counseling, is represented in *Before We Say I Do*. It is clear from these pages that Dr. McMickle has thought extensively, sensitively, and clearly about the ingredients that go into making a successful marriage.

Every pastor should read this book in order to shape his or her approach to marriage and premarital counseling. Married couples will also find its principles helpful. Mainly, I recommend it to those who are considering marriage. This resource will enable them to test how compatible they truly will be over the long haul in terms of values, commitments, beliefs, and lifestyle. Difficult as it might be (the process can also be fun and affirming), the time to discuss these important issues is now: *"Before We Say I Do."*

—*Calvin O. Butts III*
Pastor of The Abyssinian Baptist Church, New York City

Acknowledgments

THIS BOOK IS THE RESULT of working with hundreds of couples in both premarital and marriage counseling sessions in the three locations where I have served in pastoral ministry. From 1972–76, I served on the pastoral staff of the Abyssinian Baptist Church of New York City. From 1976–86, I served as pastor of St. Paul Baptist Church of Montclair, New Jersey. And since 1987, I have served as pastor of Antioch Baptist Church of Cleveland, Ohio. I want to express my thanks to the officers and members of each of those congregations for affording me the opportunity to exercise my gifts in ministry. The material in this volume is a direct result of the ministry opportunities I enjoyed with those wonderful communities of faith.

I am grateful as well to those couples whom I have counseled and with whom I have talked and cried over these more than thirty years. By the grace of God, the vast majority of those couples are still together as husband and wife—or they remained together until death parted them. Most of them have created their success, in large measure, through the premarital counseling model described herein. Marriage is the central institution of our society, and anything this model can contribute to the continued strength and success of that nurturing and mutually supportive institution finds me both humbled and delighted.

I want to acknowledge the invaluable contribution my own wife has made in the development of this model and in the strength and health of our marriage. There is nothing contained in this book that she and I have not incorporated into our own relationship. It is my deepest desire that other couples may come to know the joy and contentment Peggy and I have shared since the day we said I do.

Introduction

GETTING MARRIED is one of the easiest things in the world to do. In general, it requires only a license, a ring, and two witnesses—and some states may require a blood test. Stripped to its most basic formula, a wedding ceremony need take no longer than five minutes. But for two people to stay married for the rest of their lives is one of the greatest challenges they will ever undertake. Whereas getting married involves a single day of elegance, excitement, and encouragement from family and friends, staying married requires a lifetime of commitment, compromise, and caring about the well being of one another.

Part of my responsibility as a Christian pastor is not merely to preside at wedding ceremonies, but to explore with couples the meaning of marriage and the elements that can contribute to success in marriage. In thirty years of pastoral ministry, I have presided at the wedding ceremonies of more than one thousand couples, and I have agonized with hundreds more over the difficulties of sustaining a marital relationship. All of this has taught me one important lesson: The best time to have a discussion about marriage is before you say I do.

The nearly 50 percent divorce rate in the United States, the highest such rate among industrialized nations, attests to the difficulty of sustaining a successful, lifelong marriage. Premarital counseling can play a major role in changing this statistic, because what happens when a couple leaves the altar is greatly influenced by the preparation for marriage they receive before they stand at the altar together.

The purpose of this book is to serve as a resource for building strong marriages. I have written it primarily for couples who are considering marriage for the first time. However, its principles apply also to those who have experienced divorce and are considering remarriage. They even apply to married couples. After all, if Tiger Woods needs to consult with his swing coach during a golf tournament, then surely married couples can benefit from a resource that can help sustain their ongoing relationship.

The color of dresses to be worn by the bride's attendants, the selection of music, and the reception menu are important items when contemplating a wedding. But ultimately, success in marriage is based primarily on two factors: how suitable two people are for each other and how equipped they are to sustain the relationship that begins when they say I do. Premarital counseling helps couples to assess their suitability and to develop skills that can aid them in building a healthy, lifelong marriage.

It is rare for two people to make a perfect match as husband and wife. There will always be areas of conflict or disagreement. Through premarital counseling couples can sometimes be helped to identify those differences and learn how to accept and even embrace them. In other instances, premarital counseling can help couples recognize the differences are so fundamental that, despite the couple's physical attraction to each other, getting married could be a big mistake. Just as importantly, premarital counseling can help even the most compatible couple become aware of the challenges and tensions they are likely to face in marriage as the years go by.

I once heard a sermon entitled "Never Buy Shoes in the Morning." The preacher, Ernest Campbell, pointed out that over the course of the day a person's foot tends to swell a bit from the strain of walking and perhaps from the heat. If you buy your shoes first thing in the morning before any swelling takes place, they might not feel as comfortable by day's end.

The same principle can be applied to marriage. The true measure of a marriage's strength is not how happy the couple appears to be on their wedding day or how beautiful the bride looks as she makes her way down the aisle. Nor is it measured by the passions that engulf the couple on that first night when they consummate their marriage vows. I know of many couples where one (or both!) parties woke up the next day, looked at the person lying next to him or her, and wondered, "What in the world have I done?"

The true measure of a marriage is based on how a couple confronts and overcomes the various challenges that arise over time. Not every day will be like the wedding day. There will be other days, less magical and memorable, and more monotonous and mundane. Strong marriages are the ones in which the partners are able to find as much happiness with each other in the months and years after the wedding as they had on their wedding day. To put it another way, healthy marriages thrive as much in the midst of the routines of daily life as they do in the special moments of celebration, passion, and excitement.

This book is designed to help your marriage thrive, first by helping you discern whether or not you and your intended spouse are suitable for each other, and second, by helping you learn how to handle the pressures and problems that even the happiest couples have to face from time to time in marriage. These goals will be facilitated by focusing on seven words, each of which represents an important area or aspect of the marriage relationship. The words are *Faith, Friendship, Frankness, Fidelity, Forgiveness, Finances,* and *Family.*

Together these seven principles serve like legs on a chair that is no longer sturdy even if just one leg is removed. If a couple faces serious disagreement in two or more of these areas, they would be well advised to think very seriously about whether to go forward. For this reason, the premarital counseling method found in these pages is best used if the wedding is at least two or three months away so that arrangements that might need to be canceled can be kept to a minimum.

For those couples who choose to use this resource on their own, it is important not just to be honest with yourselves as individuals, but also to be completely candid with each other. If you avoid or suppress problems and differences today, they will most likely come back to haunt you later on. For this reason, I recommend working with someone who has premarital counseling experience. A third party is able to pick up on various comments, facial expressions, body language, tone of voice, and other indicators of disagreement or conflict, and can press both parties to explore those areas further than you might do on your own.

My hope and prayer is that you will find the ideas and principles that follow to be helpful, however you decide to proceed. I know that you are excited about your approaching wedding day, but before that day arrives, take the time to be sure that you will be able to keep the vows you are about to take. This book is based upon the premise that what happens between you and your spouse after you are married is determined, in large measure, by the preparation for marriage you receive before you say I do. I offer these perspectives with the hope of helping you to enjoy a lifelong, happy, and healthy marriage.

—*Marvin A. McMickle*

1

Faith

The First Step toward a Healthy Marriage

Do two walk together unless they have agreed to do so?
—Amos 3:3

MARRIAGE IS A SACRED UNION that should take place only after careful and prayerful consideration. The ceremony may not take place in a church, and the official license may well be on file with some agency of state or county government, but marriage is rooted in the teachings of Scripture and in the will of God.

Consider the words you will be speaking to each other on your wedding day.

The first words you will probably hear in your wedding ceremony will go more or less as follows:

> Dearly beloved, we are gathered together in the sight of God and in the face of this company to join together this man and this woman in holy matrimony, which is an honorable estate, begun by God, and signifying unto us the mystical union between Christ and the church. Which estate Christ adorned and beautified by his first miracle that he worked in Cana of Galilee. Marriage is commended of Saint Paul to be honorable among all persons, and thus is not to be entered into unadvisedly or lightly, but reverently, advisedly, discreetly, soberly, and in the fear of God.

Marriage vows are not simply words spoken by two people to each other. Marriage vows represent a pledge, sworn in the presence of God and in the presence of the witnesses who are present at the wedding ceremony, to live faithfully together as husband and wife. As you are planning for your wedding day, take some time to consider what it means to say, "We are gathered together in the sight of God." When you hear those words during your wedding ceremony, it will be important that you have considered the weight and significance of them long before your wedding day arrives.

Determine to stay in the presence of God after you are married.

You will have a better chance of enjoying a healthy, lifelong marriage when you remember always that you took your vows *in the sight of God.* In saying this I am asserting that marriage is as much an act of faith as it is a public ceremony or a legal proceeding. A license on file with some officer of the state may make you legally married, but it will be your common faith in God, in whose sight you took your vows, that will help to keep you happily married. Never forget or take lightly the significance of the words "we are gathered together in the sight of God," because *remaining* together in the sight of God is the first step on the road to keeping the vows you make on your wedding day.

It is absolutely essential that you and your spouse share the same faith perspective.

The chances of enjoying a healthy, lifelong marriage are greatly increased when you marry someone with whom you share a common religious tradition and a common routine of religious life and practice. You may remember the Broadway play and subsequent Hollywood film *Fiddler on the Roof.* Based upon the writings of Isaac Beshiva Singer, that wonderful story centers on the importance of husbands and wives sharing a common faith tradition. It is the tale of a devout Jewish milkman who has five daughters for whom he hopes to find good husbands. The oldest daughter marries a nearly destitute tailor who, despite his poverty, is an established member of the Jewish community in their small Russian village. The young couple is married beneath a canopy with the local rabbi presiding. There are shouts of *mazel tov* all around.

Another daughter wants to get married to a young man who is visiting the village, but who lives in the distant city of Kiev. This young man wants his bride-to-be to leave the little village and live with him in the city. The father is heartbroken about having his daughter move away and live so far from the rest of the family, but the man she loves has already returned to Kiev and she is determined to be at his side. While the young man is of a revolutionary frame of mind, he too is a faithful Jew who has affirmed his faith and lived out its rituals and commandments.

The story then turns to the third daughter who announces to her father that she wants to marry a young man who is a member of the Russian Orthodox Church. Her father flatly refuses to give his blessings to that idea, and he goes so far as to disown her as his daughter when she disobeys him and marries "outside the faith." It appears that the couple has been married by a Russian Orthodox priest. Did the Jewish girl convert to the Orthodox faith, or did the priest marry them despite the fact that they were of two different faith traditions? That question goes unanswered in the tale.

What does not go unanswered in this story is whether or not a shared faith tradition is something that a couple must consider before they get married. I strongly contend that it is. Sharing a common faith tradition is the first and most important step toward a successful marriage. The words of Amos apply to you and to your marital relationship: "How can two people walk together unless they agree?" Be sure both of you agree that marriage is a deeply spiritual relationship, and be sure that both of you agree that sharing a life centered on your common faith in God will be central in your marriage.

Faith is not just how and where you worship God; it is the glue that holds your marriage together.

The role of faith cannot be overstated in terms of its ability to affect the success or the failure of a marriage. How couples respond when they face unexpected setbacks can be greatly influenced by whether or not they share a common religious tradition. You may want to pray about a problem that has arisen in your marriage, but your spouse may not see the worth of that activity. Or, your spouse may want to turn to the Bible for guidance in some areas of decision-making, but you may actually prefer to consult with someone who practices the occult (e.g., horoscopes, zodiacs, tea leaves, palm readers, mediums, or tarot cards).

How you respond to each other when one person has said or done something that has hurt, offended, or embarrassed the other person is informed by whether or not you share the same faith tradition. One of you will want to talk about forgiveness, reconciliation, or confession. Meanwhile, the other person may be more concerned with revenge or blame or never trusting again. How you raise your children, how you spend your leisure time, how you invest your money, and how you plan for your future are all issues that are affected by the role that religious faith plays in your life and in your marriage.

Be sure that you and your spouse establish your marriage on a shared spiritual foundation.

In an article entitled "Secret to Marriage: Spiritual Foundation," David P. Gushee speaks directly to this point. He says:

> The biblical understanding of marriage is covenant relationship binding a man and a woman to each other for life. Marriage is an exchange of promises in which two individuals freely bind themselves to each other and promise to behave in a way that will bring blessings rather than curses into each other's lives. Marriage is a covenant, and it is for life. Do not marry someone who does not believe this.

He continues:

> Ground your relationship on spiritual and moral commitments. It is impossible to maintain one's marital vows apart from a deeper set of religious and moral commitments. To use the language of my own faith community (while acknowledging that others use different language), commitment to

another person must be rooted in commitment to Jesus and to a life of following him as Lord.[1]

Think of marriage as a "one-flesh" relationship wherein your two lives are inseparably bound together.

There are two verses in the Bible that speak about the spiritual foundation by which marriage is understood. In Genesis 2:24, marriage is defined primarily by the words "and they will become one flesh." This same image appears again in Ephesians 5:31. This is not only a powerful biblical and theological concept, but it is also a beautiful visual image of what life together should look like. When two people become "one flesh" it ought to be difficult if not impossible for them to be separated from one another. When two people have become one flesh, no third party can intrude into that relationship from the outside. When two people have become one flesh, no third party will be invited into the relationship from the inside. When two people have become one flesh, the foundation for a lifelong marriage has been established, and divorce becomes an unlikely and unacceptable outcome for that relationship.

Jesus speaks about the strength that should be evident in marriages based upon this one-flesh concept when he says in Matthew 19:6, "Therefore, what God has joined together, let man not separate." This concept of "one flesh" will be referred to over and over again throughout this study. It is widely agreed that this image seeks to describe not only the physical union between a husband and a wife that takes place in moments of intimacy, but it also speaks of the spiritual union that is the essence of marriage. All of the remaining steps in this seven-step methodology are based upon this opening assumption. Only when two people become "one flesh" can they enjoy the fullness of marriage. Nothing can be hidden or withheld when two people become one flesh. No problem has to be faced alone when two people become one flesh.

Marriage is more than a legal relationship; it is primarily a covenant relationship with God and with your spouse.

As was mentioned by David Gushee, marriage can also be understood as a covenant relationship wherein you and your spouse commit yourselves to each other for the rest of your lives.[2] When you get married you will always be seeking the other's best interest. You will always love, honor, and cherish each other. You are promising to be loyal to each other in every sense of the word. There is no other person on earth with whom you will exchange the kind of vows that will join you to your spouse. There is no other person on earth to whom you will make the kind of promises that you will make to your spouse. There is no job, no fraternal group, no political organization, and no church auxiliary with whom you will ever exchange such words as "for better or for worse, for richer or for poorer, in sickness and in health, to love and to cherish until death do us part."

Marriage works best when God is at the center of both of your lives.

Note that I said that you will have no other relationship *on earth* as close as the one you will have with your spouse. It must be understood that your primary relationship must be with God, and not with your spouse. As much as you love your husband or wife, you must love God more than that. Only then can God be the head of your life and the center of your home and marriage.

In his book *Lasting Love: How to Avoid Marital Failure,* Alistair Begg sets forth an observation that I strongly urge you to consider before you say I do. He says:

> When we think about relationships, we should be very clear that our relationship to God must come first.... Are we seeking first the kingdom of God and endeavoring to do the right thing, or are we just living to please ourselves? Until we settle this matter, we are unprepared to make the right decisions about other relationships.[3]

Begg suggests that part of having a right relationship with God is possessing a spiritual perspective on such things as material possessions and what we in American society refer to as the pursuit of happiness.[4] When you and your spouse are on the same page concerning these things, your marriage has an increased likelihood of being a happy, lifelong relationship.

Now consider what happens when you are not both on the same page. One of you wants to seek the "abundant life" mentioned by Jesus in John 10:10, and the other one wants to pursue the "good life" as defined by John Locke and regularly encouraged by *The Wall Street Journal* and *The Lifestyles of the Rich and Famous*. It is easy to see how persons who are pulled in such different directions could have difficulty in living happily ever after.

"Unequally yoked" describes the difficulty of being married to someone with whom you do not share a common spiritual foundation.

While the warning in 2 Corinthians 6:14 about not being unequally yoked together was not spoken by Paul in relation to the institution of marriage, it serves as a useful metaphor by which the role of shared faith within a marriage can be considered. Paul created an image of two different types of work animals—perhaps an ox and a mule—that are yoked together and set to work in a field as a team. Obviously those two animals have little in common and would be hard pressed to work together effectively. Paul then suggested that believers and unbelievers would have an equally difficult time working together as a team, because they reflect some fundamental differences. Paul placed on us as believers the bulk of the responsibility for avoiding "fellowship" with persons who do not share our faith commitment. In fact Paul went even further by quoting Isaiah 52:11, "Come out from it and be pure."

Paul was obviously speaking in the context of a Christian minority living within the cultural context of the Greco-Roman world. He was fighting the battle of establishing the faith within the nascent Christian community in Corinth, and he believed that the faith would have a better chance of taking root if these recent converts were not constantly in the presence of non-believers. Paul was urging the Corinthian Christians to be careful about the company they kept; fearing that it was possible for the values and behaviors of those non-believers to compete with, and perhaps even to contradict the very things that he was trying to teach them.

Paul was not directing his comments directly to the question of whether believers should knowingly enter into marriage with non-believers. In fact, in 1 Corinthians 7:12-14 Paul acknowledged his own awareness that such marriages had taken place within that community. Paul was aware, however, that married life can become enormously complicated when you and your spouse are not united in this aspect of your lives. Consider just a few of the areas that can be affected when husband and wife do not share the same faith perspective.

A popular tune with two different sets of lyrics highlights what it looks like when you and your spouse do not have a common spiritual foundation.
During the height of the Motown Records era, Gladys Knight and the Pips released a best-selling song entitled "You're the Best Thing That Ever Happened to Me." Not many months later the equally popular gospel singer James Cleveland took the same melody and many of the same lyrics, but he made one telling change to the song. He called his version "Jesus Is the Best Thing That Ever Happened to Me." These two songs point to a fundamentally different way of viewing the world, one that centers on Saturday night and the nightclub scene and the other one that centers on Sunday morning and the church. One speaks of staying out late on Saturday until the last dance is over, and the other wants to be at the 8 A.M. service the next morning.

Of course the husband and wife can have a healthy appreciation for both songs, dancing together on Saturday night and praising God together on Sunday morning. It is also possible for couples to share in each other's world with a little effort, even if they are somewhat divided in their preference for Gladys Knight or James Cleveland. The concern being raised here is what happens to a marriage if the husband and wife are going to live on different tracks most of the time. With one person heading out of the house on the way to church while the other person has just returned to the house after a nightlong round of clubs and cabarets, marital bliss may be harder to achieve.

Without a common spiritual foundation, conflict will likely arise around involvements in the church concerning both time and money.
The two most immediate challenges for married people who do not share the same faith commitment will likely involve disagreements over the time and money that one party wants to invest in church life without the support, or over the resentment of the spouse.

Time. Consider first the issue of time. While one of you wants to go to church, the other one wants to stay in bed or go to a Sunday brunch. While one of you wants to attend a midweek prayer service or revival meeting, the other wants to go to a movie or attend a concert. While one of you wants to participate in a choir rehearsal or church auxiliary meeting, the other wants to go bowling or spend time at home with friends. It will be hard to build a life together when you are moving in different directions and following different schedules.

It is precisely this problem of being a married, couple pulling in two different philosophical directions that Lee and Leslie Strobel discuss in their book, *Surviving a Spiritual Mismatch.*[5] In their case, neither was a Christian when they got married, and they enjoyed a lifestyle where Sunday was for brunch at the mall or breakfast in bed. Then Leslie was converted to an evangelical faith in Christ, and that brought enormous strains upon their marriage. Those strains did not end until Lee also gave his life to Christ some ten years later. (By the way, his decision for Christ was earnest and sincere and not done simply to appease his wife.)

Before you say I do, and before you begin what is meant to be a lifelong journey with your intended spouse, be sure that differences in your faith commitments will not have the two of you pulling in opposite directions. You may try to accommodate those differences for a while. One of you may attend church at the other's urging, and one of you may pretend not to mind that your spouse jokes about being a "bedside Baptist"—one who says he or she believes in God but stays in bed Sunday after Sunday. These concessions will not last forever, and eventually your respective core values will resurface and the two of you will find it harder and harder to walk together because you do not agree in this all-important area of married life.

Money. A similar set of concerns surrounds the question of the use of household funds when you are divided over matters of faith. Suppose one of you strongly believes in generously supporting the church through financial donations, while the other person feels that such generosity is not only poorly invested, but takes away from your ability to enjoy a more comfortable lifestyle? More will be said about this issue in the chapter dealing with finances. Suffice it to say at this point that, if one of you insists on tithing one-tenth of your income to the church over the strong and constant protests of your spouse, you are sowing seeds of resentment and unhappiness. Whenever something cannot be done because of financial concerns, the money that one of you spent on church-related activities can become a regular flashpoint of controversy.

Money directed to church support is not the only instance where disagreements can arise. It is just as likely that couples who do not share a similar faith perspective can disagree on how to spend their money when it comes to the normal expenses of daily life. One of you may feel that building wealth and long-term financial security is the number one priority for the family. The other may be informed by the words, "Seek first his kingdom and his righteousness, and all these things will be given to you as well" (Matthew 6:33).

One of you may feel led to direct large amounts of the family income to charities and relief work, because you are informed by Jesus' teachings about "the least of these" in Matthew 25:31-45. The other may be more informed by a narrow view of the notion that "charity begins at home." When two people do not agree on something as fundamental and foundational as faith in and faithfulness to God, it is likely that they will also not agree on how to allocate their time and their money.

Another area of conflict likely to arise if you and your spouse are "unequally yoked" will be the role of spiritual values in the home.

The challenges faced by couples who are not equally yoked extend not only to what happens outside the home (church attendance and stewardship), but also to many things that happen within the home they share together.

Will your spouse offer a prayer before sharing meals together? Will you read Bible stories to your children and pray with them before they go to bed? Will Christmas be observed simply as a secular season of the year defined by gifts and gaiety, or will the biblical meaning of that holiday be incorporated into the family celebration?

I have seen husbands and wives sitting together in the church when their child has a part in the seasonal Sunday school pageant, but no such mutual interest in spiritual issues is displayed in the home. If you travel a different path outside the house in terms of active church involvement, and also follow a different path in the house in terms of daily family devotional activities, there is not much on which both you and your spouse may agree that can offset the foundational differences you have in this area of life. If one of you is active in the church while the other one is apathetic, perhaps even openly hostile toward religion, that is a serious warning sign that the two of you may not be suitable for marriage, no matter how physically attracted you are to each other. How can two walk together unless they agree?

Persons deeply committed to their Christian faith are wise to avoid interfaith marriages.

The terms *believers* vs. *unbelievers* so far as the gospel is concerned are not the only way in which this problem of being unequally yoked can present itself. It can be equally challenging if both parties are devoutly religious, but follow widely divergent paths of religious life. America is a diverse society in terms of religion, and it is becoming increasingly common for people to choose to follow the example of the third daughter in *Fiddler on the Roof* by marrying across lines of religious difference. Christians are opting to marry persons who are Muslim, Jewish, Buddhist, or adherents of lesser-known religious traditions.

It is rare for a third party simply to say no to an interfaith couple intent on getting married. Love and passion have a way of crowding out reason and reality. People in love are certain that "love will conquer all." Perhaps they are right, but they better be aware of just how much "all" there will be for them to conquer if both of them choose to take their faith traditions seriously after they have been married.

The issue is not so significant if both persons are only nominally involved in their faith traditions. There are few compromises to make or conflicts to resolve if neither person sees religious affiliation as essential to his or her personal identity. People who attend church, synagogue, mosque, or temple only on rare occasions and who never bring their religion home with them are not likely to encounter the normal challenges that await those couples where both persons take their differing religious traditions seriously and where they are going in separate faith directions on a regular basis.

Which traditions will be observed in your home? Will a Christian husband want to share in and be supportive of his wife's observance of the Muslim's month-long fast of Ramadan? Will a Jewish wife be open to preparing her husband's favorite meal even if it includes pork chops? He can, of course, prepare the meal for himself as a way of getting around that issue, but it points to the many areas where differences can arise. How easily can the Hanukkah menorah and the Advent wreath occupy the same house? The same can be said about the annual convergence of Passover and Easter. It may seem as if these holidays overlap from a calendar point of view, but there is no overlapping of the theology that is involved.

What are the challenges when the Quran and the New Testament do not agree on the question of "who is Jesus?" Will a bell be struck at the beginning of Buddhist chants in the same house where the other spouse is haunted by the words of Joshua 24:15, "As for me and my household, we will serve the LORD"? If you are serious about your relationship with Jesus Christ, and I certainly hope that you are, then you need to understand how complicated your life becomes when you marry someone who is equally committed to an entirely different faith tradition.

Who will preside at your wedding? The conflicts begin even as the couple is standing at the altar. Will a rabbi and a pastor jointly preside at the wedding ceremony? Shall an Imam be invited to say a prayer in Arabic and offer a reading from the Quran? This issue can be complicated enough when a Protestant and a Catholic decide to get married, but even more fundamental differences arise when the ceremony involves a Christian and a non-Christian. You could always elect to have a secular ceremony with no religious language or symbolism, just to keep peace in the house. To do so, however, is to make a real statement about the role and importance of faith in both of your lives. This is quite a lot for love to conquer, and an interfaith couple needs to seriously consider "all" of this before they decide to get married.

What lessons will be passed on to children? It may be possible for an interfaith couple in love to face these challenges together and try to work out whatever theological differences may divide them. There still remains the question of what values and traditions they will pass on to their children. Will the Jewish spouse press for circumcision, bat or bar mitzvah, instructions in the major annual holidays, and attendance at the local synagogue? Will the Muslim spouse want to encourage the children to engage in prayer five times a day even if the other parent in the home is praying within an altogether different tradition? Will the non-Christian parent understand the desire of a Christian spouse to have their child christened or baptized, and will the non-Christian parent participate in or be absent from those joyous events?

As said before, if you are willing to compromise on your faith commitments as a condition for getting and remaining married, it is entirely possible that you will also compromise on these questions about child rearing as well. However, if one of you takes your faith seriously and the other does not, what does the believing spouse do with the idea in Deuteronomy 6:7, which says about the commandments of God, "Impress them on your children. Talk about them when you sit at home…"? Whose views will be passed on to the children?

In most successful marriages the persons involved share the same worldview, meaning that their personal values and their social views are largely the same.
Fran Dickson of the University of Denver has done studies that show the positive impact that having a common "relationship vision" has on success in marriage. She argues that "when there is a shared belief system—including mutual understanding about the meanings of life, death, and marriage—it's likely to be easier to develop a relationship vision."[6] Four other researchers make a similar point when they say:

Since it is fairly likely that the religious feelings of spouses

tend to be similar, among the more religious, who probably
come from religious homes, there may be a supportive complex of perceptions leading to increased marital satisfaction.
That is a shared worldview.[7]

The question is what constitutes a worldview or a relationship vision
when there is no shared faith between the persons involved?

See if you and your prospective spouse are able to agree on the issues listed below.

Another group of marriage experts offers a short list of complex moral
questions that can complicate any marriage that is not anchored by a
common worldview.

- Sanctity of life versus choice and freedom: Is abortion OK?
- Personal responsibility versus community responsibility: Why do
  people do wrong?
- Capital punishment: Is the death penalty ever appropriate?
- Responsibility toward your fellow humans, animals, and the
  environment: How do we help care for and protect the world in
  which we live?
- Sexual behavior: What is appropriate? Why? On what do you base
  your judgment?
- Drug or alcohol use: What's OK with you? Why?[8]

To this list could be added several other issues that are reflective of
your spiritual worldview, or the worldview of your spouse.

- Birth control practices
- School vouchers vs. public schools
- Issues of war and peace
- Attitudes toward persons of different racial or ethnic groups
- The role of women in ministry
- Gun control and weapons in your home
- Pornographic materials
- Charitable giving and philanthropy vs. greed and self-indulgence

You and your intended spouse need to review these issues together
and honestly determine your level of agreement or disagreement on
this short list of topics that have divided people across this country

and around the world. You do not really know each other until you know how your partner feels about issues such as these.

Amos 3:3 asks the question that you need to raise with your intended spouse before you say I do. The King James Version renders it this way: "Can two walk together, except they be agreed?" You may not always agree on what television shows to watch or what to have for dinner or where to spend a family vacation. Your marriage can easily survive all of those disputes so long as you are in solid agreement on the things in life that are truly basic and foundational.

Do you agree that Jesus Christ is Lord? Do you agree that an active church life will be at the center of your life together? Do you agree that the teachings of Scripture will guide and inform the decisions that you will make in every area of your lives? Do you agree there is power in prayer and that you both will lay hold of that power by regularly praying together? If you agree on these things it is likely that you will enjoy a long-term, healthy, and happy marriage!

It only makes sense that God should be at the center of your marriage, and that faith should be the first of the seven steps that contribute to success in marriage. After all, your marriage begins on that day when you hear these words: "We are gathered together in the sight of God...."

Questions for you to consider

1. Is God at the center of your life? If so, how are you making your selection of a spouse in light of your relationship with God?

2. Are you considering marriage to someone to whom you are physically and emotionally attracted, but with whom you do not share a common faith tradition? Why or why not?

3. Do you agree that your marital relationship is strongest when both you and your spouse have a living and vibrant relationship with God that involves your public times of worship and your private times of devotion and daily decision-making? Why or why not?

4. Do you view marriage as primarily a legal matter sanctioned by the state, or as a spiritual union based either upon the "one flesh" concept or upon the idea of marriage as a covenant partnership? Why? What are the implications of your view?

5. Do you believe that a shared religious faith is essential for a healthy, lifelong marriage? Why or why not?

6. Have both of you shared openly about the role that religion plays in each of your lives and about the role you expect your religious faith will play in your life together? If not, do so now.

7. If your spouse-to-be told you that he or she did not share in your religious faith and would not welcome such issues into discussions concerning how your life together should be directed, would you still choose to marry that person? Why or why not?

8. Do you and your spouse share the same worldview? Do you generally agree on the issues discussed on pages 14–15 of this book? If not, how will you resolve your differences?

9. What problem would it pose for your marriage if your spouse wanted to invest more time or money in church activities than you thought was reasonable?

10. Are you determined to raise your children within your faith tradition, and does your spouse share in that conviction? If not, what are the implications for your relationship?

2

Friendship

When Home Is Where Your Heart Is

Two are better than one, because they have a good return
for their work:
If one falls down, his friend can help him up.
But pity the man who falls and has no one to help him up!
—Ecclesiastes 4:9-10

ONE OF MY FAVORITE late-night television shows is the 1960s
classic comedy series called *The Honeymooners*, starring Jackie Gleason
as Ralph Kramden. In one episode of that comedy series, Ralph has
talked his friend Ed Norton into withholding their rent because the
landlord of their Brooklyn, New York, apartment building has decided
to raise the rent by $5 per month. The landlord responds to their rent
strike by turning off the heat in their respective apartments even
though it is the middle of winter. Both men and their wives wrap
themselves in coats and blankets and decide to stay inside their
apartments so they cannot be served with an eviction notice.

Late one night there is a knock on Ralph Kramden's door, and he
discovers that Norton is standing in the hall. With his usual boisterous
tone, Ralph asks Ed why he has left his apartment. Ed responds by
saying, "I didn't mind having no heat, no hot water, or eating cold
food, but three days alone with my wife was more than I could
stand." Norton was willing to pay the rent increase if for no other
reason than that it would keep him from having to stay one more
minute alone in the apartment with his wife.

One of the keys to a solid marital relationship is when you are perfectly content to be alone with your spouse.
That scene from *The Honeymooners* points to one of the realities of married life. There will inevitably be those occasions when a husband and a wife will be together with no other friends or family for long periods of time. Those can and should be among the happiest and most rewarding times of your marriage. It may occur at the end of any average workday. It may happen during vacation times, while traveling together by car, or when inclement weather prevents you from getting outside for hours or even days at a time. Unless you have taken the time as a couple to develop a genuine friendship with each other above and beyond any sexual attraction you may feel, those hours together can be long and hard to endure. That is why it is essential that a marital relationship be undergirded by a solid friendship.

The strongest marriages usually involve couples that are each other's best friend.
One of the surest indicators of the strength and health of your marriage is the knowledge that you and your spouse are each other's best friend. This friendship between spouses exceeds the mere fact of spending time together as all of us might do with other people on the job or in a variety of social settings. There is a deeper level of trust and devotion associated with your best friend, and no one should enjoy more of your trust and devotion than your spouse. William Shakespeare once said, "Love all men but trust only a few." This observation relates well to the difference between your relationship with your spouse and your relationships with other friends and acquaintances. No one should receive more of your love or trust than the person to whom you are married. That is what makes that person your best friend.

There is one question dealing with this issue of friendship that I ask every couple with whom I do premarital counseling: If you were to be deserted on an island with just one other person for an indefinite period of time, who would you wish that other person was? Of course, an occasional smart aleck will choose Jesus Christ or Babe Ruth or their laptop computer with a wireless Internet connection. The fact is, however, that the answer to that question takes us right back to *The*

Honeymooners and to Ed Norton not being able to spend three days alone with his wife.

Far beyond being physically and emotionally attracted to one another, a strong marriage requires that you also "like" the one you love.
What does the word love mean to you? What are you saying when you tell your future spouse that you love him or her? What are you understanding that person to mean when he or she speaks those words to you?

So complex and profound is the word *love* that in the New Testament there are three different words used to express our one English word. There is *eros,* which speaks of erotic or romantic love. There is *phileo,* which speaks of brotherly love or friendship. Finally there is *agape,* which speaks of the unselfish, sacrificial, and self-giving love shown to us by God who "so loved the world that he gave his one and only Son, that whoever believes in him shall not perish but have eternal life" (John 3:16).

Add all three of these feelings together and you begin to understand the kind of love that one spouse should feel toward the other. Love is not any one of those emotions; it is all three combined into a warm and wondrous feeling that you share with only one other person on earth. As the old song so aptly says, "Love is a many splendored thing."

Eros. Most couples do not need much explanation when it comes to *eros* or the passion of sexual attraction and fulfillment. You are probably already dealing with the power and appeal of this particular passion. It was this strong desire to share a time of intimacy with another human being that led Paul to recommend that some people should get married: "It is better to marry than to burn with passion" (1 Corinthians 7:9). This is the language of poets and songwriters. But be cautious about this face of love. No matter how strong this feeling may be rising up within you, you are ill-advised to marry someone simply because they "turn you on." "Until death do us part" is a very long time, and the fires of passion alone are not sufficient to sustain your marriage for that long.

Phileo. You also have to like the one you love. Plainly stated, your spouse should be as attractive and interesting to you when he or she is fully dressed as when you are both naked with romance on the mind. That is where *phileo* comes in and reminds us that the love that takes the form of friendship with each other is just as important as that aspect of love that takes the form of sexual desire. Your spouse should not merely be your lover; your spouse should also be your partner and companion in the other areas of life as well.

Do you remember your younger years in high school or, perhaps, in college when you could not wait to be with your friends? Do you remember how you would spend hours together during the day and evening and still talk on the phone late into the night? Do you remember how you planned all week for what you would do together when the weekend finally came? If anyone were to ask you why you did that you would answer by saying, "Because those are my friends." Time always went by too quickly when you were with your friends. You could barely wait until your classes or workday was over so you could once again be with those friends.

The same sense of affection that you shared with your dearest friends when you were growing up is precisely the affection you should be able to give to and receive from your spouse. It is that feeling of love as *phileo* that will send you home every night, rather than being drawn away from home and spouse to spend most of your time with others. If you and your spouse are not each other's best friend then you will both probably spend more time with whomever your best friend is than you will with each other. Do not let this happen in your marriage!

Agape. It must be said, however, that a long-term, healthy marriage requires more than passion and friendship. It also requires an unhesitating willingness to sacrifice your time, money, and effort to aid or assist your spouse. Just like the love that God showed toward us when God gave us the best he had in Jesus Christ, so should spouses always be willing to give each other the best they have to give, even if that means they have to sacrifice something they wanted for themselves in order to meet the needs of the other person. Unselfish love is crucial if a marriage is going to last for a lifetime.

I remember one cold and blustery winter day when my wife and son had traveled with some other parents and children to a hockey tournament in Niagara Falls, Canada. I was working on my doctoral dissertation at the time, so I remained behind. On the way back from the tournament, the car in which they were riding broke down, and since it was a Saturday evening the parts needed to repair the car would not be available until the next Monday morning. Meanwhile, they were all in Niagara Falls, more than three hundred miles from home.

I was sitting at home by a warm fire, hard at work on the dissertation when the phone rang. My wife and son were stranded, and she needed me to get them. I did not remind her of the work I was trying to accomplish. I did not tell her how comfortable I was sitting by the fire back in Shaker Heights, Ohio. I told her that I would leave at once, and that I would be there as quickly as possible. That was not *eros* at work; that was *phileo* and *agape* at work in our marriage.

God has shown unselfish and sacrificial love toward us, and we should willingly show that same kind of love toward each other. Be sure that your spouse is not only your lover *(eros)*, but also your best friend whom you love *(phileo* and *agape)*, for whom no sacrifice is too great.

A healthy, long-term marriage requires that you value who your spouse is on the inside and not just how he or she looks from the outside.
Physical attraction is one of the primary forces that draw two people together. We are quickly and easily enamored with such things as body shape, facial appearance, bust size, a muscular physique, hair texture, and the subtleties of eyes and smiles. There is an old adage about beauty being only skin deep. I associate that phrase with a song from the Motown group, *The Temptations*, who sang about a person who judged his loved one beyond outward appearances.

My friends ask what do I see in you,
But it goes deeper than the eye can view.
She's got a pleasing personality,
And that's an ever-loving, rare quality.

At the beginning of your marriage the outward physical appearance of your spouse is a significant part of his or her appeal. It is important to discuss what it is about your spouse that arouses your passions. Many individuals work very hard to maintain those outward features in order to be continually attractive to their spouses. What must be remembered, however, is that outward appearances are subject to change whether by the ravages of disease, the passing of time, or the trauma of an accident.

What will hold your relationship together after weight gains are not so easily lost? What will keep you two together after a mastectomy or impotence has affected not only your physical body and your psychological well-being but also your intimacy as husband and wife? The stronger your friendship becomes over the years, the easier it will be for you to navigate the physical changes that will have a direct impact upon your marriage.

Be prepared to tell your spouse that you do not love only his or her body parts—that you love every aspect of his or her existence—mind, sense of humor, habits, and idiosyncrasies. Somewhere between saying I do and the day when death parts you, you *and* your spouse will go through many significant changes, many of which will directly impact those outward features that may have initially drawn you to each other. Only those couples who have moved beyond being only lovers to have established a solid friendship as well will be able to sustain a healthy and happy marriage in the midst of all of those changes.

The strongest of friendships are sustained by a multitude of common areas of interest.

When contemplating marriage you should consider how many common interests you share as a couple. Do both of you enjoy the same kind of music, the same kind of recreational activities, or the same kind of food? Can you sit together and enjoy the beauty of nature or cuddle up together and watch a program on TV? Can you sustain a simple conversation that flows from one topic to another and never get tired of simply being together? Are there projects around the house that you can both work on, even if you bring different skills to that task? "Until death do us part" is a long time, and it can feel even longer if the two people involved share few common interests.

Neil Clark Warren has set up a Web-based system known as

eharmony.com that seeks to determine whether or not a couple has enough common interests to sustain a lifelong marital relationship. In speaking about his approach to premarital counseling Warren says, "Opposites may attract. But if you want a lifetime of love, the truth is quite the opposite. A soul mate is someone with whom you experience a lot more similarities than differences.... Over the long haul, it's similarities that make a marriage joyful."[1]

I am convinced that the success of my own marriage is due in large measure to the fact that my wife, Peggy, is unquestionably my best friend. I am also convinced that our friendship is the result of a wide range of common interests. Both of us were raised during the years when Motown Records, James Brown, and Aretha Franklin were at the height of their popularity. We sing those old songs together and laugh at the things we remember doing when those songs were first released. We watch all of the TV shows about "The Golden Oldies of Soul Music."

That has served two useful purposes. First, it reminds us of our individual pasts, and as we talk about those years we get to know more about each other and how we became the persons that we are today. Just as significant, however, is the fact that we are sharing time with each other today and building common memories that continue to bind us together into the future. Friendship begins with common interests, and couples need to be sure that they have that foundation to build upon.

Many things can serve as points of common interest in your marriage, and the more of them you have, the better it will be for your marriage.
The list of possible common interests is virtually inexhaustible, and the more of them that you share with your intended spouse, the better it will be for your marriage. A short list could include such things as bowling; playing cards and board games; home decorating; watching movies at home or in the theater; various forms of physical exercise and recreational sports; participating in political activities; attending museum exhibitions and other cultural institutions; sharing in religious activities in the home, at church, or at a retreat location; dining out; visiting and caring for seniors and persons who are shut-in;

traveling together, whether for a day or longer; sharing in a book club or an investment club; dancing; entertaining friends at home; gardening; watching news programs and talking about current events; supporting groups and programs that deal with civil rights and other social justice issues; listening to radio programs; shopping for antiques; attending classes and special lectures at area colleges; and following local sports teams, whether in person or on TV.

One sure sign of a solid friendship is when you are willing to share in the specific interests of your spouse even if those things are of no particular interest to you. It is most unlikely that two people will share everything in common. Part of the mystery of romance and relationship is discovering the things that are unique about your spouse and demonstrating a willingness to share in the things that are of special interest to your partner even if they are of no real interest to you whatsoever. Marriage requires compromise and accommodation when it comes to learning how to handle interests that are not common to both persons. By definition, something that is an interest in a person's life is likely to involve time, money, and maybe even space in the house or apartment. The willingness to support each other's particular interests is a key indicator of a healthy relationship.

Sometimes Peggy shares in my personal interests. One of my great passions in life is planting and caring for flowers inside and outside our house. My wife does not have a similar passion for gardening, but she is more than willing to support my interest. On hot days she brings me a cold drink and a snack when I'm out in the garden. Three or four years ago we went to the garden center together and purchased a particular flowering vine known as a clematis. When we brought it home she helped me dig the hole, put down the peat moss, and place the plant in the ground. Now we enjoy watching those purple blossoms appear every summer, knowing that the plant was the result of her sharing in one of my interests.

Turnabout is fair play. One of Peggy's great passions is home decorating—and shopping for the items to complete a project. I do not share her passion for this activity, but I often go with her to the stores to pick out the things she needs. Not only do we buy the items in question, but we also enjoy talking in the car as we travel back and forth from home. Quite often a shopping trip will involve lunch or dinner together, and so we have more time just to be together.

Many times she will do the purchasing alone, but I enjoy seeing what new things she has done to make our living environment more beautiful and comfortable for both of us to enjoy. I handle the roses and she handles the rugs. I take care of the flower boxes and she buys the furniture for the deck. Then we sit on the deck furniture that she purchased to enjoy the flowers I planted. Neither of us shares the other's passion at this point, but we enjoy the fruit of each other's labors.

Newlyweds can learn a lot about building a marriage on friendship by looking at the successful marriages around them.

There are many couples in our congregation who have been happily married for fifty years or more. It is apparent to everyone who observes these couples that they are each other's best friends. It is also apparent that they not only have an abundance of common interests, but they gladly support and share in those things that are of interest to their spouses.

Several older women participate in a quilting circle every Thursday morning. It is more than a time to produce beautiful quilts that they either sell or give away; it is a wonderful way for them to spend several hours together as sisters in Christ. However, on any given Thursday morning there are several husbands who are seated in that room as well. They have not come to do any quilting. They are just supporting an activity that is important to their wives. Younger couples would do well to learn from this example of showing an interest in and supporting a spouse's involvement in activities that are important to him or her, even if the activities do not interest the other person at all.

True friendship allows and even affirms some areas of difference.

One of the most unlikely marriages in America is between two high-profile political activists, James Carville and Mary Matalin. On the surface, they would appear to have nothing in common. He was the chief strategist for the presidential campaigns of Bill Clinton, and he is the quintessential "liberal Democrat" who goes so far as to represent that point of view on the CNN show *Crossfire*. She is a hard-core "conservative Republican" who served as a strategist for both Ronald Reagan and George Bush. On all things political they seem to be on the opposite side of every issue, and yet they remain happily married to each other.

I do not know how they manage this balancing act in their marriage, but I would strongly encourage couples contemplating marriage to view this Washington, D.C., "power couple" as the exception to the rule and not as an ideal model of how to assess compatibility with a potential spouse. Some differences in temperament, experience, taste in music, or preference in food when dining out can make your relationship more interesting. Friendship in marriage does not require that you and your spouse be carbon copies of each other on every significant issue. Sometimes it is the areas of difference that add spice to your marriage.

However, these differences should not carry over into every area of life or else there will be nothing upon which to establish a relationship. Many couples have learned to live with and learn from the subtle differences they have with each other, even when it comes to some social or political issue. In short, do not panic when you do not always agree on everything so long as the list of things on which you *do* agree is long.

If you truly value your spouse you will respect the fact that occasionally he or she needs to be alone.

Even the best of friends need some time to be alone with their thoughts and those interests in which the other person chooses not to share at all. Like many men in America I am a sports enthusiast during all seasons of the year. This is one area where my wife has little, if any, interest. I also like to smoke an occasional cigar, and this is something in which she is really uninterested. She, on the other hand, enjoys talking on the telephone with family and friends around the country for long periods of time. She also loves to listen to the various speakers and music on Christian radio stations. She times both of these practices to coincide with the time I spend glued in front of the TV watching Tiger Woods or the Cleveland Indians or as many college football and basketball games as I can squeeze into my schedule. Not only do we love to be together, but we also understand and accept each other's need to be in separate parts of the house doing different things. Everybody needs some "space" from time to time.

I lead a hectic and stressful life filled with a crowded writing schedule, meetings and classes, phone calls, office visits, and hospital calls from morning to night. When I get home at the end of the day I need some time to wind down, and for me that works best either on the deck of our home or in the study I have created in the basement. It is a time to reflect on the events of that day, and it is also a time to get ready for the challenges of the coming day. My wife understands the need I have to be alone for this purpose, and she respects that time.

By the same token, I often enter into a room looking for her and find her cuddled up with the Bible or some other type of devotional reading. I have learned to quietly turn around and leave the room without saying a word, respecting the fact that when she is talking with God, any conversation or activity that is on my mind at that moment is likely to be a distraction. Whatever I have to say can usually wait for a later time.

You can measure the depth of your friendship by the time the two of you spend talking about matters of broad interest—which should greatly exceed the time you spend complaining about problems in your relationship.
One of the best signs of a healthy relationship is the qualitative and quantitative time a couple spends sitting and talking to each other. In a book entitled *Fighting for Your African American Marriage*, coauthored by four experts in the field of family and marital counseling, the point is made that one of the most important things required to maintain friendship within marriage is taking plenty of time just to talk. The couple does not have to go anywhere or spend any money. All they have to do is share time with each other talking about anything that is on their minds.[2]

The four authors suggest that an unhealthy friendship finds a couple only talking about the problems that have arisen within the relationship. In contrast, healthy friendships in marriage allow the conversation to cover a wide range of issues that have nothing to do with those problems.

These two observations from that book summarize both sides of the issue about talking as the key to friendship in marriage. The first section offers a glimpse of the topics that are frequently discussed in a healthy friendship.

> Friends talk about sports, spiritual matters, politics, perceptions of the world, philosophy of life, humorous anecdotes in the families, fun things they have done or will do, dreams of the future, and thoughts about what each person is going through at this point in life.[3]

Couples should be concerned if, in contrast, all they ever talk about are the problems and pressures in their relationship.

> Some of the common subjects are problems with the kids, concerns about who can take care of Mama, problems with too many bills and not enough money, problems with getting the car fixed, concerns about who's got time to get some project around the house done, problems with figuring out who is going to see the kids' teacher for a conference....[4]

The authors suggest that the preoccupation with problems and concerns tends to increase after the initial thrill of getting married tends to fade. They state:

> If couples aren't careful, most of their talks end up being about problems and concerns—not about joy and fun. Problems and concerns are part of married life, and they must be dealt with, but too many couples let these issues crowd out the other, more relaxed talks they once shared and enjoyed.[5]

When couples are accustomed to talking with each other on a wide range of subjects on a regular basis, there is an increased likelihood that any problems that might arise can be addressed more quickly and more candidly. The problem becomes just one of the many things they will discuss that day. More often than not, the problem will not even be the last topic they will discuss; hence it never seems that the only thing they talk about are their problems.

Never forget that in a marital relationship little things mean a lot. Try to surprise each other with a small act of kindness or affection every chance you can.
Friendship in marriage, like friendship in any other setting, must be nurtured and cultivated. Let your marriage be strengthened by the unexpected gestures of love and thoughtfulness that can bring a smile to the face and joy to the soul of your spouse. Of course it is important to remember birthdays and the wedding anniversary, but friendship reaches beyond those two conspicuous events. Very few wives, if they have primary responsibility for preparing the evening meal, will turn down an invitation to go out for dinner and then go to the movies. Very few husbands, if they are sports fanatics, would not welcome some small item that bears the logo of their favorite team. Of course, to avoid any charges of sexism or stereotyping, both of these examples work just as well when the husband does most of the cooking and the wife follows the activities of a favorite team or sports player!

You may be each other's best friend, but try to understand and allow for the importance of the other friends that may be a part of your spouse's life.
The fact that your spouse is your best friend should not in any way preclude the presence of other close friendships that are enjoyed by the husband and wife together or separately on the job, within a social circle, or in connection with some special interest. Marriage should not be viewed as the cut-off date for all other friendships—past, present, or future. Sometimes a newly married person may be jealous of the time that his or her spouse spends with other friends. Some balance must be found so that it is clear to everyone that one's spouse comes first in terms of time, loyalty, and affection. However, it is a sign of a healthy relationship when husbands and wives can be refreshed by the nurturing friendships they maintain outside of their marriage.

This means that friendships born of a sorority or fraternity connection are valuable and important. Friendships based upon participation in some sports league should not be viewed with suspicion or
resentment. Friendships on the job that involve eating lunch as a
group or getting together periodically after work are a normal part of
the human experience. As long as it is clear to everyone involved that
such gatherings and associations will never be allowed to take prece-
dence over your commitment to your best friend (your spouse), these
other friendships should be encouraged and accepted without any
anxiety about what the other is doing when you are apart.

You may be joined together on your wedding day, but you will have to work every day for the rest of your lives to stay together.

One of the most popular soul singers of the 1970s was Al Green, and
one of his biggest hits was entitled "Let's Stay Together." Staying
together is easier to do when the couple actually spends time *together!*
This can include such simple things as sitting close together while
watching TV or reading or even while traveling.

I often share the story I heard about two couples who were driving
along a street in two different cars. In one car the person in the front
passenger seat was leaning against the door on that side of the car, and
there was no physical contact between that person and the driver of
the car, not even hands or shoulders. As they came to a stop at a red
light they were sitting behind a car in which another couple was riding,
and this couple was sitting so close together it seemed as if they were
sitting in the same seat. The passenger in the second car said to the
driver of that car, "Do you remember when we used to sit that close
together?" The person sitting behind the steering wheel then observed,
"I never moved."

When love is young and passions are flowing freely, couples tend
to reflect the pattern of that couple in the first car. They want to be
close together. In a healthy marriage they work hard at staying
together. However, if they are not careful, over time they will
become like the couple in the second car, confined to the same space
but not connected to one another in any meaningful way. One or

both of them will have "moved." My advice to couples is always the same: Try to *stay together*. This is not hard to do when your spouse is also your best friend.

Questions for you to consider

1. Is there anyone other than your spouse with whom you would prefer to spend most of your leisure time? If so, who and why?

2. Is your intended spouse also your best friend? If not, who is your best friend and how does that person fit into your life?

3. Is there anything you own or any resource you possess (e.g., time, money, knowledge, experience, business or professional contacts) that you would not be willing to share with or sacrifice for the sake of your future spouse? If so, what and why?

4. What are the things, beyond outward appearance, that you find attractive and appealing in your partner?

5. Try to name 10–15 things that you have in common with your intended spouse that can serve as the foundation upon which your lifelong relationship can be built.

6. Are there any areas of apparent difference that you know you are going to have a hard time accepting or living with? If so, what are they?

7. Are there any things about your intended spouse that are going to have to change in order for the marriage to be successful? If so, what are they?

8. Are you likely to get jealous if your spouse wants to spend some time with other friends from the job or from some other social circle in which you are not involved? Why or why not?

9. Are there any friendships that you are going to have to sever once you get married, because you know they might intrude upon your marital relationship? Why or why not?

10. How long can you be away from your intended spouse before you start to miss him or her?

3
Frankness
Speaking the Truth in Love

Instead, speaking the truth in love, we will in all things grow
up into him who is the Head, that is, Christ.
—Ephesians 4:15

**It is very important that both of you feel you
have "permission to speak freely."**
In the military a lower ranking person cannot openly question the
conduct, judgment, or commands of a superior unless and until that
person is given "permission to speak freely." The military is not a
democracy in its organizational structure. It is built upon a unified
chain of command that flows from the top down. Orders are given
and obeyed without question or hesitation.

You must never allow your marriage to become like the military
where either one of you has to keep thoughts, questions, and opinions
to yourself. That is why the third step to a healthy marriage is building
a relationship that allows for frankness on the part of both parties.
Both you and your spouse must constantly feel that you have permission to speak freely.

A healthy marriage requires that both of you can speak openly,
honestly, and sometimes critically about what is happening in your
relationship. If you and your spouse share a common faith, and if you
are also bound to each other through a solid friendship, you can and
should feel free to tell your spouse whatever is on your mind pertaining
to your life together.

Do not let the sun go down on your anger.

There should never be the fear that by telling your spouse what is on your mind you might be endangering the relationship. Both parties need to understand that there will be those times when disagreements will rise, when feelings will be hurt, and when tempers might even flare. In such moments, what is needed is open and honest dialogue. You are not doing yourself or your marriage any good by bottling your feelings up inside yourself. Those unexpressed emotions will come out sooner or later, and it might take a more explosive shape simply because, like a carbonated soft drink inside a can or bottle that has been shaken, there was no way to relieve the pressure that was building inside.

Two biblical verses in Ephesians 4 shed light on the importance and value of frankness. One is Ephesians 4:26, which says, "Do not let the sun go down while you are still angry." The other is Ephesians 4:15, which refers to "speaking the truth in love."

Verse 26 deals with the times when you and your spouse should speak frankly with one another. It is always better for your relationship if matters of genuine concern can be discussed sooner rather than later. You may attempt to hold in things that are bothering you, but more often than not, the issue keeps churning inside you because you feel hurt, offended, or taken for granted. Whenever possible, try not to go to sleep until you have discussed with your spouse those matters of concern that have arisen between you that day. The night can be long, and the usual intimacy and playful exchanges that normally take place within a healthy marriage can quickly be replaced by a cold shoulder, cutting comments, and an air of tension that can be cut with a knife. When you feel free to discuss whatever is on your mind, however difficult it may be for the other person to hear, it is likely that the concerns can be addressed and the normal relationship between you and your spouse can be restored.

Beware of the practice of conflict avoidance that results in your failure to maintain open communication with one another.

The reason for a failure to engage in open communication is usually something known as conflict avoidance. Whether you are doing it knowingly or unknowingly, one of you is refusing to discuss the problem or conflict that confronts you. Perhaps you think that by avoiding any discussion of the problem it will simply go away. If the issue was significant enough to cause some tension in your marital relationship, however, then it is safe to say that it will *not* go away simply by avoiding discussion of it. Perhaps you are concerned that if you engage in a discussion of the problem you may say something that will hurt the feelings of your spouse or vice versa. The fact is, if you engage in conflict avoidance, *what you refuse to discuss today will probably erupt a few days later, and the chances of saying or hearing something hurtful will only have increased.*

Practice Paul's principle of speaking the truth in love.

The other verse, Ephesians 4:15, focuses on the spirit in which your much-needed frank conversation should take place. When disagreement or dissension rises, it is always best if the matter is addressed right away. However, no matter how touchy the issue may be and no matter how strongly either of you may feel about the issue, a healthy marriage involves two people who are *more interested in reconciliation than in rebuke.* Therefore, the tone of the discussion should be civil and low-key. The use of violence, intimidation, threats, or hints at reprisals of any kind, which are far too common in the world today, should never surface.

When those kinds of responses do occur while you and your spouse are attempting to discuss matters of difference and disagreement, recognize such behavior as an area of your relationship that needs serious and immediate attention. Remember: *the truth is spoken in love.* Just as importantly, remember that the truth is also being spoken to the person with whom *you are in love.* Mutual love should always inform the tone and tenor of even the most frank exchange.

Let your marriage be governed by the Golden Rule.

The best way to approach a frank discussion of a problem in your marriage is to ask the question, How would you like to have someone bring this matter to your attention if you were the one being addressed? Permeating biblical faith is the invitation to love others as you love yourself. The Golden Rule says, "Do unto others as you would have others do unto you." That is an appropriate way for you and your spouse to speak frankly to one another without being hurtful or overly harsh. Speak to your intended spouse as you would like to have your spouse speak to you on any matter of conflict or disagreement.

No issue should be "off limits" when it comes to frankness.
The need for frankness may come into play in any number of circumstances in your marriage. You need to be able to communicate openly and candidly about your financial concerns and about how your financial resources should be spent or preserved. You need to be able to discuss your views and approaches to child rearing, especially where issues of discipline are concerned. This chapter highlights areas where frankness and candor are essential. Once again, you need to have a discussion of these issues before you say I do.

You should feel free to discuss all issues related to your health, past and present.
Nothing should be hidden or withheld in this area of life, because it is likely to become known later on, and when it does the lack of honesty and candor earlier in the relationship can become a serious problem. Past medical procedures, existing medical conditions, and pending medical treatment should all be revealed prior to the marriage. That level of frankness should continue if and when medical problems arise once you have exchanged your marriage vows.

The range of possible medical concerns that can have a direct impact upon a marriage are wide. Many people suffer from a variety of mood-related disorders ranging from depression to schizophrenia, from bipolar disorders to premenstrual syndrome. Couples later in life may deal with various forms of sexual dysfunction or reproductive disorders. Chronic diseases such as asthma, diabetes, arthritis, sickle cell and other anemic conditions, urinary tract infections, and recurring neurological conditions should be revealed and openly discussed. Additional health-related concerns are identified individually below.

Chemical dependency. Any previous history or present struggle with chemical dependency (drugs or alcohol) should be revealed prior to the marriage. It is unfair to withhold from a future spouse information about behaviors and addictions such as these that have the potential to dramatically affect your marital relationship. If the dependency has been overcome, a spouse can serve as a continuing source of support for the person who is learning to live without some substance he or she once abused. If the dependency is continuing and perhaps still being concealed from the future spouse, it will become known eventually. This behavior cannot be hidden forever. It will come to light either as a result of being unable to account for missing funds or household items that are being used to acquire drugs, or as a result of the visible, physical effects of substance use and abuse.

In today's environment, chemical dependency involves both legal and illegal substances. Inquire about such illegal drugs as crack and powdered cocaine, heroin, marijuana, and any of the new synthetic drugs that are now available. However, it must be understood that the number-one substance of chemical dependency in America is alcohol. Millions of people in this country are alcoholics, and millions more have to live with the affects of alcoholism every day. Be honest with each other on this topic. Do not duck the issue, because drug addiction and alcoholism are nothing to play with. They have destroyed countless lives and ruined untold numbers of marriages in the past. Discuss this issue before you say I do!

Sexual intimacy. You must be able to speak frankly with one another about things that relate to the physical intimacy that you will share as husband and wife. Both of you may not come to the marital bed with the same set of previous experiences, or with the same set of expectations. What takes place between consenting adults in the context of a healthy marriage is a gift from God that can be enriching for both persons. However, both persons should feel free to speak frankly about things they do and do not enjoy, and about behaviors and activities they will and will not perform. This aspect of married life is too important, especially early in your new life together, to feel that you cannot say what is on your mind about that aspect of your relationship.

Sexual history. A related concern is the question of a person's sexual history. In an age when it is less and less likely that both persons will enter marriage after a lifetime of celibacy or abstinence, it is important for both of you to know each other's sexual history. This is not done simply to pry into the past for no substantive reason. It must be understood that with the rise of sexually transmitted diseases (STDs), there is no such thing as a harmless one-night stand. Infections that can be contracted through sexual contact can be passed on by further sexual contact. Couples need to know what risks they face when they are intimate with one another.

Consider getting an HIV/AIDS test before you get married.
When I got married in 1975 couples were still required to take a blood test before a marriage license could be issued. This was done to test for the very things I am suggesting here—most especially syphilis and gonorrhea. It seems strange to me that at a time when such diseases are spreading rapidly through the population that a blood test is no longer universally required. I think this is a mistake, especially in a world where the dreaded condition of HIV/AIDS is killing tens of thousands in this country alone and millions around the world.

Given the fact that HIV/AIDS can lie dormant for up to seven years before it attacks a person's immune system, the discussion about sexual history must reach back at least that long. This can be a difficult discussion for some people to have, because they may be revealing a shocking level of sexual promiscuity. Anyone who has recently attempted to give blood through the American Red Cross knows that organization has become particularly sensitive in this area. You and your spouse need to be equally frank with each other on this aspect of intimacy.

Be sure to discuss any same-sex acts in which either of you may have been engaged.
Anyone who has attempted to donate blood to the American Red Cross knows full well that before you can do so you must answer a battery of questions about same-sex activity. The Red Cross is not merely prying into your life; it is trying to protect other lives by protecting the nation's blood supply. Such is the world we live in today. You need to discuss these same kinds of questions before you say I do.

Even a single instance of same-sex activity should be revealed, because the consequences of that event can come back to haunt you many years later. Take the time to discuss your respective views of same-sex activity to be sure that you agree on this controversial issue. Some people can live a bisexual lifestyle without their spouses ever catching on to their double life. However, like all other secrets that we try to keep from our spouse, this one has the potential to leak out in one way or another, and when it does it can have devastating consequences on your marriage.

I have known several women who lived with and later died from HIV/AIDS-related illnesses. In each instance, these monogamous women contracted the virus from their spouses who were engaged in bisexual activity. In the urban centers of America where most of my ministry has taken place, that practice of male bisexuality is called "the down-low." Men who engage in such practices are known as "down-low brothers." Whatever it may be called in your community or culture, be honest about any such activity in either of your pasts. Perhaps there will have been not a single incident by either of you. But, given the continuing spread of HIV/AIDS in our world, this is a question well worth pursuing.

Be honest *now* about any children you may have conceived in earlier marriages or past relationships.

The existence of any children conceived in earlier marriages or with former lovers should be revealed, because you can never be sure if or when those children might be standing on your doorstep. Take the time to consider how the children from that previous relationship are going to factor into your new life together. Who is going to have custody of those children? How often will they be visiting the home where you and your intended spouse will live? Is there likely to be any contact with a hostile former spouse when those children are dropped off or picked up for a visit?

Getting married is complicated enough, but when you are walking into the ready-made family of spouse and children from earlier relationships, the time needed to adjust to that new life increases considerably. This is a world of blended families where both spouses are bringing with them into a new relationship the children of former relationships. Such blended families are no less complicated, however, for being commonplace. That being said, you should be open and honest about your feelings in this area.

Let me be explicit in emphasizing that a premarital discussion about intimacy in marriage should not be limited solely to the question of what awaits you as you share that part of married life together. It must also necessarily include an honest discussion about your past practices, because what you do not know *can* hurt you.

Discuss your individual housekeeping habits and preferences.

Housekeeping habits or the lack of them can become a source of tension fairly early in a marriage. Try to agree on things that may sound simple but which, if left unaddressed, can become matters of considerable tension and conflict. Should the bed be made up every morning and who is going to do it? How often should the kitchen be cleaned and the sink cleared of all dishes? Will that task be shared by both parties in the marriage? If there is a pet, who will care for it? Where will telephone messages be left so they reach the person for whom they are intended?

These things seem small, but when two people have been living in separate places for any period of time prior to getting married, how they share their living space once they begin to cohabit together as husband and wife becomes very important. There must be the ability to communicate on aspects of life together that are of concern to either party. This becomes more important if the space in which you live is small and confined. For example, some people have the luxury of having a closet or storeroom where things can be put out of sight until it can be decided whether or not to throw them out. However, when that kind of space is limited, you need to be mindful about stacking and storing things in a way that irritates you or your spouse.

Some people are fastidious and want to maintain an immaculate and orderly living space. Other people don't mind moving old news-papers and stacks of junk mail just to find a place to sit down in the living room. Two such people can live happily ever after together as long as they know what they are getting into, and as long as they are willing to make some concessions to their spouse in the area of housekeeping. Just be aware that housekeeping habits die very hard, so you had better know what you are getting into before you say I do.

The saga of the socks. This dichotomy of housekeeping habits reflects my own experience in marriage. When Peggy and I first got married, I had a habit of leaving my socks at the side of the bed where I took them off every night. I also had the habit of getting up the next morning and leaving those socks right there with no particular thought about her housekeeping habits. For the first few weeks she patiently picked up those socks and put them in the hamper with no questions or comments. Eventually she confronted me about it and asked me if I would either put my socks in the hamper at night before I went to bed, or take them with me to the hamper when I got up the next morning.

I didn't really hear what she was trying to say; she did not want to be responsible for picking up my dirty socks every day. Of course, I had been leaving my socks by the bed for days at a time for the preceding ten years before we got married. It never bothered me, but it annoyed her to no end. Once more she asked me to remove my socks from the bedroom. I gave her a hug and a kiss, told her how sorry I was, and promised to do better.

Needless to say the habit continued. When she brought it up again I told her again that I was sorry. When I went to hug her as I had done before and blow off her concerns, she took my words and turned them back on me with an entirely different nuance. "You are sorry," she said to me, "you are one sorry person."

I got the point. It was candid. It was frank, but it was effective. I still take off my socks and leave them beside the bed each night, but I put them in the hamper every morning. Now I am not nearly as "sorry" as I used to be.

Be candid about any prior involvements with the criminal justice system.

As sad as it is to acknowledge this, the number of men and women who have been arrested and even incarcerated for a felony offense is steadily increasing. There are nearly two million people in this country who are currently incarcerated. There are many more who are presently on parole or pre-release. It is probably a chapter in their lives that these people would like to put behind them. However, it is not a chapter that can be kept undisclosed from your future spouse. Given how our society views and treats ex-felons, it is inevitable that this issue will surface at some point in the future. It is far better to be honest about it from the outset, rather than have it come to light after the marriage has taken place.

It is very likely that people with felony arrests and convictions earned that dubious distinction as a result of some involvement with illegal drugs. Such persons may have been nonviolent offenders more in need of drug treatment than incarceration. However, as more and more states seek to give the impression that they are getting tough on crime by locking up all drug offenders, the number of people who will likely become saddled with a felony arrest continues to escalate.

In many states across this country, ex-felons cannot exercise the right to vote. That is certainly an undue hardship on the person who has paid a debt to society, but it also becomes one of the ways by which a felony record can come to light. If individuals have not been honest about this chapter in their lives, they have to account for their non-participation in the voting process in one way or another. A felony record follows you into almost every employment office you enter. Increasingly, the acknowledgement of a felony arrest, to say nothing about a felony conviction, can be enough to keep a person from ever securing steady employment. That has long-term implications for a couple that may want to apply for a mortgage loan or engage in any other large financial undertaking. In short, a felony record is not something that can be kept hidden, especially from your spouse, so it pays to be frank and honest about this issue before the marriage takes place.

Frankness in speech must be received as well as it is offered.

Most people are much better at speaking frankly to another person than they are at listening to and accepting frank and honest comments directed at them. It is one thing to get something off your own chest by telling your spouse exactly how you feel about a certain issue.

However, in a healthy marriage the channels of open communication always work in both directions. It is as important for both persons to demonstrate a willingness to hear what their spouse has to say to them as it is for them to feel free to speak whatever is on their mind.

It is usually obvious when you are attempting frank speech on a topic that is difficult for another person to hear and receive. The party on the receiving end of frank talk wants to hurry up and end the discussion. Often they will not make eye contact. They will typically try to argue back in their own defense and seek to demonstrate that they are not deserving of what is being said to them. They may try to shift blame back to the spouse who raised the issue, or to another person altogether.

It is difficult to sit down and listen carefully when someone is honestly sharing a concern about our conduct or attitudes. Nevertheless, it is crucial that frankness be seen by both persons as a two-way street where the truth can be spoken in love and received in humility, without any concern about putting the future of the relationship at risk.

Frankness before you get married can greatly reduce the risk of divorce.

I contend that many divorces could have been avoided and that many unhappy marriages could have been transformed into healthy relationships if the people involved had chosen to confront their problems and conflicts with frankness and honesty. Couples too often talk about their spouses with third parties rather than talk openly to their own spouses about matters of importance. Marriage is not just about those moments of "better," "richer," and "in health"—those times when everything is going well. Marriage is about working through the ups and downs of human relationships: "for better *or* for worse, for richer *or* for poorer, in sickness *and* in health." The ability to speak with frankness to each other is a crucial ingredient in establishing and sustaining a healthy marriage. If your marriage cannot stand under the weight of frankness, it is doubtful that your marriage will last very long at all under the weight of time.

Consider the best context in which you can have a truly frank discussion.

It may not be necessary for your premarital counselor to sit in on and hear all the details that may come up in such discussions as are being suggested here. It may be sufficient that the counselor raise the importance of frankness as an area that you and your spouse need to address between yourselves. The downside of not having such a discussion during a premarital counseling session is that there is no guarantee that such a discussion will ever take place at all. You and your spouse may choose to overlook or gloss over the areas where conflict is likely to occur. In those instances, an objective third party can guide you through difficult discussions.

On the other hand, especially when issues of intimacy and sexual history are discussed, if a counselor is present there is no guarantee that both of you will speak as freely and as honestly as needed if the discussion is to be useful. Proceed in this area with caution.

Questions for you to consider

1. Do both of you feel that you can speak freely with each other on any topic? Why or why not?

2. Are you willing to be governed by the principles from Ephesians as discussed in this chapter: to never let the sun go down on your anger and to speak the truth in love? Why or why not?

3. Have you had a frank and honest discussion about such matters as your health, finances, and sexual history? If not, create time and space to do so soon.

4. Are you aware of each other's housekeeping habits? Are you prepared to live in the same house with each other's habits? If not, what habits will need to be modified?

5. Will you be as willing to receive candid comments as you might be to give them? If not, why not?

6. Will you continue to consider these topics whether or not you use a third party to lead you through this discussion?

4
Fidelity
What Does It Mean to Forsake All Others?

For this reason a man will leave his father and mother and
be united to his wife....
—Genesis 2:24

ONE OF THE MOST IMPORTANT MOMENTS in your wedding
ceremony occurs when you consent to the exhortation "...forsaking
all others...." This phrase serves as the basis for what is meant here by
fidelity. The term *fidelity* carries several layers of meaning. It means
"faithfulness; the careful observance of duty or performance of obli-
gations or vows; or a firm adherence to a person or party with which
one is united or to which one is bound." This dictionary definition
applies perfectly to the meaning of fidelity in the context of marriage.
It is essential that both of you understand the meaning and importance
of fidelity as one of the keys to a healthy and successful marriage.

**One of the ways to think about fidelity in marriage is
to consider the phrase "I pledge allegiance...."**
Most Americans are familiar with the concept of fidelity outside the
context of marriage. Fidelity or loyalty is what is at stake when we
speak the words "I pledge allegiance to the flag of the United States
of America...." In speaking those words, we commit ourselves to
faithfulness, duty, and adherence to something with which we are
united. We are aware of fidelity in the political sense, which involves
keeping faith with our country and not allowing any third party to

undermine that allegiance. What a married couple must do is appreciate the need for a similar kind of allegiance between themselves in the context of their daily life together.

. The phrase "forsaking all others" points you and your spouse in that direction from your very first day as husband and wife. Marriage demands faithfulness, the careful performance of vows, and a firm adherence to the person to whom one is bound. As with issues of loyalty and allegiance where the nation is concerned, couples contemplating marriage need to understand the absolute necessity for loyalty and fidelity within their relationship, and they must also understand the many ways by which the issue of fidelity can be understood.

Marriage can and should alter all of your other relationships.

When you get married you are, in effect, altering all the other relationships with which you have been engaged up to this time. In some cases, some serious, earlier relationships will have to be ended altogether. Other social relationships will have to be redefined. When you get married, your primary allegiance shifts—away from parents and peers, away from siblings and various social acquaintances, and even away from narrow questions of personal self-interest—to your spouse.

From the moment you say I do, you are entering into a covenant relationship with each other that makes your relationship with your spouse unlike any other relationship in your life. Once you say I do, your primary allegiance is to one another, and that allegiance, that loyalty and fidelity, must stand "for better or for worse, for richer or for poorer, in sickness and in health, for as long as you both shall live."

Infidelity involves much more than you may think.

Both of you need to be alerted to the various ways by which your fidelity to each other can be undermined. The concept of fidelity in marriage has typically focused on the issue of monogamy or of avoiding any extramarital affairs. And it is true that such sexual infidelity can be a grievous offense that has the power to undermine the most promising of marital unions. However, when a young couple is considering marriage, this form of infidelity is not the most immediate threat to their union. Therefore, if the meaning of fidelity stretched no further than the single topic of monogamy (i.e., sexual fidelity), then, frankly, there would be little urgency in discussing the topic prior to the wedding day. The fact is, however, that there are many other circumstances far more likely to present themselves early in your life as a newly married couple that can have just as poisonous an effect on your relationship as adultery.

The first challenge of fidelity is staying together "for better or for worse."

Every day of married life will not be romantic and exciting. There will be those occasional stretches of time when life takes on a certain predictability. There will be meals to prepare, laundry to wash, bills to pay, and various household chores to perform. There will be the demands of work and probably the demands of raising children. In the face of all of this, there will be precious little time and even less energy for anything else. Marital vows become the glue that holds couples together during those times of busyness.

It is hard to imagine on your wedding day that one or the other of you, looking radiant and alive, can suddenly become sick, incapacitated, bed-ridden, and even permanently disabled. When you are dressed up in wedding gown and tuxedo with flash bulbs going off and family and friends looking on adoringly, it is easy to imagine that every day of married life will be like your wedding day. Remember that the words of the wedding vow, "for better or for worse, for richer or for poorer, in sickness and in health," are specifically designed to point you beyond your wedding day. They point you on to those other days that await you as husband and wife when you will be challenged to keep the promises you made to each other when you stood at the altar and said I do.

Fidelity means that when those times do come in your marriage, you have every reason to believe that both of you will have each other's support and allegiance throughout whatever changes and challenges you are facing. Sexual fidelity may never be an issue in your marriage, but sickness, unexpected setbacks, and the predictable stresses and strains of maintaining a household are sure to occur along the way. Fidelity asks the question of whether or not your spouse can count on you to keep your word and honor your marital vows when those hard times come your way.

Always remember that times change and so do people.
In a wonderful book entitled *The Many Loves of Marriage*, Thomas and Nanette Kinkade talk about the role that wedding vows play in the life of a successful marriage. The two people involved in a marriage are constantly changing over time, whether in terms of their appearance, their health, their ideas, or their goals and aspirations. The world around them keeps changing, causing the couple to redefine and reconsider their future in terms of employment, income, place of residence, or family living arrangements. Among the very few things that remain the same over time are the wedding vows. The Kinkades write:

> Wedding vows speak of unchanging realities in a world that reinvents itself with every passing hour. The promises you made to each other, in time and space, before the solemn scrutiny of the eternal God and the witness of family and friends remain. The vows precede the multitude of mysteries in a marriage and go with you through those mysteries.[1]

I am convinced that divorce rates would fall drastically and the number of healthy and happy marriages would increase dramatically if couples would only keep faith with each other and with themselves where the words contained in the wedding vows are concerned.

The problem seems to be that the words spoken when many couples get married do not result in the creation of "unchanging realities in a world that reinvents itself with every passing hour." Even in the absence of anything as unpleasant as adultery, too many couples seem willing to end their relationship at the first sign of trouble. What did they think it meant to say "for better or for worse"? Will you be determined to keep your wedding vows once your wife no longer fits into a size-eight dress, or once your husband has lost his hair and maybe even his virility?

Times change and so do people, and you need to consider the full range of changes that can and most likely will take place during your married life. You will not always have as much time to be together as you have at the beginning of your married life. You may discover that you do not agree with each other on some social or political issue, and if you feel strongly enough about your views on that subject, there is the possibility for real stress in the relationship. Your marriage vows can pull you through all of that if you are determined to practice this broader definition of fidelity.

Roughly 50 percent of the couples who exchange marriage vows and pledge allegiance, loyalty, and fidelity to each other are unable or unwilling to keep those vows. Prior to your wedding day, you need to be challenged to consider this issue. You need to be challenged to practice this form of fidelity in which you keep faith with yourself and with your spouse where the wedding vows are concerned. When you get married you are making a sacred promise to each other in the presence of God, and you ought to work as hard as you possibly can to keep that promise "for better or for worse." Fidelity to the wedding vows is what holds you together as a couple in the face of an ever-changing world that is consciously and unconsciously pulling you apart.

Consider whether you value anyone's opinion more than that of your spouse.

There is another aspect of fidelity that needs to be considered, and it has to do with whether or not you will allow the opinions and suggestions of others outside of the marriage to outweigh the opinions and suggestions of your spouse. These opinions can be introduced into the marriage from one of two directions. First, people can offer unsolicited advice, and second, we can turn to certain persons for their advice or opinions. Neither of these occurrences is bad, and in fact, both of them occur in the healthiest of marriages. The question is what you will do with that input from other people when you know it conflicts with advice and opinions you have received or will later receive from your spouse? Whose opinion will matter most, your marriage partner's or your golf partner's?

It is entirely possible that your golf partner or coworker may be able to offer very sound advice on a matter that is under discussion by you and your spouse. It is possible that the suggestions being offered by that third party are far more prudent or practical than anything being suggested by you or your spouse. The question is not the value of the advice being given by a third party; the question is what to do with that advice when it is discovered to conflict with views that are expressed by your husband or wife. In a healthy marriage, husbands and wives take the time to consider together the third party opinions that come their way. The couple may both come to see the wisdom of the advice given to them by a third party. The danger comes when one person feels that his or her opinion as it pertains to issues that affect the marriage matters less to the other spouse than the opinion of some person outside of their marital relationship.

Listen most closely to the person with whom you have chosen to live the rest of your life.

I have made the mistake in my own marriage of paying more attention to the voice of a third party than I did to the voice of my own spouse. I allowed the sales pitch of a real estate agent to persuade me to purchase a home over the expressed concerns of my wife. To her credit and my great relief, my wife had a love for me that was deeper and more lasting than that disappointment that I dealt to her in 1987. Our marriage has survived that lack of fidelity on my part, and we continue to live in that house fifteen years later, after having made many changes and improvements. I deeply regret having listened more closely to the voice of a third party than I did to the voice of my wife. I have encountered that real estate agent only occasionally in the intervening years, but with my wife, I have been living with and within the consequences of that decision I made despite her expressions of concern.

It must be remembered that the most important covenant relationship that you will ever be engaged in, outside of your relationship to God, is with your spouse. No one else has to live as directly with the consequences of your actions and decisions. When you make a decision based on your mutual input and your reciprocal trust and confidence in each other, neither of you will feel left out of the process. When a decision is made based upon the input of a third party over the objections of your spouse, the principle of "one flesh" is once again being undermined. Other voices can be invited to share in the decision-making process, but in a healthy marriage you and your spouse ought to reach the final decision together!

The list is long of people who will offer you their opinion, but be careful about taking those opinions too seriously.

The list of third parties who can offer solicited or unsolicited advice can be quite long. A short list would include fraternal and church group members, coworkers, in-laws, siblings, and neighbors. It can include newspaper advice columnists, radio and TV talk-show hosts and guests, and the other media personalities who seem to know how to fix whatever is wrong in someone else's life. Other predictable settings for opinions—often unsolicited and usually unwelcome— would be barbershop and beauty salons where the problems of the world are regularly addressed during a wash and set or a haircut and a shave. This list even includes pastors and other counselors who often believe that their advice should be taken as law and gospel.

In cases of specialized information such as financial planning and taxes, real estate transactions, medical care and legal procedures, you would do well to seek out expert third-party opinions. However, even in the case of specialized knowledge, you ought to consider that information together with your spouse, rather than having one of you and an expert third party make a significant decision over the protest of your spouse or without his or her participation in the process. That expert third party will likely not be around the house when the door is shut, the lights are turned off, and an angry or annoyed spouse is left to wonder why his or her views and opinions matter so little in the marriage. Proceed in this area with great care.

Remember that you are married to your spouse and not to your children.

I completely agree with the words of Psalm 127:3 that say, "Sons are a heritage from the LORD, children a reward from him." One of the greatest gifts and one of the most awesome responsibilities that God can bestow upon a married couple is the gift of children. More will be said about the impact that children can have upon marriage in the chapter on family. The reason children are being discussed in the chapter dealing with fidelity is to make the point that many couples allow the relationship with their children to become more important than the couple's relationship with each other. Children are a gift to marriage, and as such they should be viewed as an outgrowth of, but not an alternative to, the relationship between the husband and the wife.

Being a newlywed is not a guarantee against becoming a parent.

It must always be remembered that the possibility of newlyweds becoming parents is always present. Regardless of what natural or clinical birth-control methods you may use, you may be surprised to discover that an unplanned pregnancy is about to alter your established plans in some significant ways. You must take seriously the possibility of pregnancy and parenthood, and more importantly you must understand how that development can alter your relationship to your husband or wife.

Children can be all-consuming as far as time, money, energy, and emotional involvement are concerned. The demands children can place on a couple are both immediate and constant. From the moment they are born, children alter the relationship between the husband and wife, especially when it comes to having uninterrupted time together. As the years go by, the demands of parenting do not lessen; they only change as the child grows from one stage of life to the next. In the face of this reality, it is important that you work at maintaining the core relationship with your spouse. The most important thing that parents can do for their children is to maintain a loving, nurturing, and supportive relationship between themselves, allowing the children to grow up inside a stable family relationship.

Consider what will happen to your marriage when "the nest is empty."

You want to be careful that you never allow your relationship with your children to supplant in importance the covenantal relationship you are maintaining with your "one-flesh" partner, your spouse. Some couples, who have allowed their relationship with each other to wither away over time, suddenly find themselves remaining together only because of the children they have in common. In other words their children, and not their loyalty to each other as agreed to in their wedding vows, have now become the glue that holds that marriage together. Then the inevitable day arrives when the children move out of the house, the empty-nest syndrome sets in, and the husband and wife have no one else to focus on but each other. If that core marriage relationship has not been sustained and kept strong during the years when the children were in the house, that marriage is likely to collapse as soon as the children are gone. I have seen this happen over and over again.

A solid relationship between a husband and a wife is the best ingredient to bring into any parenting role. No matter how much you will come to love your children, when you stand together on the day of your marriage you are pledging allegiance, loyalty, and fidelity to your spouse. In so doing, you are forsaking all others who might come between you and your spouse, and that must also include the children who may come along sooner or later. I married my wife Peggy on June 7, 1975. Our son Aaron was born on May 12, 1980. He effectively moved out of the house in September of 1998 when he went off to college in New York. Peggy and I continue to live "happily ever after" largely because we love each other first and we love our son together.

An essential aspect of fidelity is being able to keep each other's secrets.

It is a sign of a healthy marriage when both parties feel comfortable sharing with each other the deeply personal and private details of their past and present lives. However, what is revealed inside the marriage relationship should be held in strictest confidence by that couple and should not be shared or discussed with others outside that covenant partnership. Fidelity also involves being trustworthy and reliable when it comes to a couple being able to keep each other's secrets.

There are things that a married couple shares with each other that must not be shared outside the trust and confidentiality of that covenant partnership. The couple may share information with each other about health-related problems. They may share candid concerns about the conditions of their employment. They may choose to reveal some feelings about a member of the extended family. They may disclose some action or conduct that occurred before they got married about which they continue to be ashamed. They may decide to confess to each other certain fears, doubts, feelings of inadequacy, or personal failures that are affecting their self-esteem.

Couples may find themselves going through a variety of personal crises. It could include such things as their financial situation, problems that involve their children, potentially embarrassing physical conditions, or legal issues of one type or another. If one person desires not to have any of these things shared with anyone else outside the marriage, that desire should be honored and that personal problem should be kept between the husband and the wife. Of course, if both parties agree to share it with others on a selective basis, that is perfectly acceptable.

There is an amusing TV commercial for a product that relieves constipation that speaks to this problem. A woman is sharing with a friend the discomfort her husband feels from this particular problem and she pulls a bottle of milk of magnesia from her purse. The poor husband is mortified that such a personal problem is being so casually shared with others. He begs her to put the bottle away and to change the subject, but the discussion goes on and on and on. When we see something like that happen in a TV commercial involving paid actors, it gives us a laugh. When we do it in real life and it brings hurt or embarrassment to our spouse, it is no laughing matter.

In the motion picture *The Green Mile*, Tom Hanks plays a prison guard who is in charge of the cellblock where the electric chair is housed and where executions are carried out. The term *mile* refers to the distance of the corridor from the cellblock to the execution chamber, and in this case that corridor was painted green. Many things were said and done on "the mile" that involved both prisoners and prison guards. However, there was a clear and consistent rule that applied to everyone involved: "What happens on the mile stays on the mile." No one who operated inside that setting shared anything that happened there with people who operated outside that setting.

A similar rule should apply within marriages. *What happens in the marriage stays in the marriage.* Obviously this would not include acts of physical abuse. I am not suggesting that either party should suffer in silence while being beaten or otherwise harmed or humiliated by a spouse. I am also not suggesting that individuals should remain silent about violations of the law by a spouse, which could make them complicit if such violations were to come to light. But in terms of the daily events and conversations that define married life, fidelity should be the rule, meaning that both parties can speak in confidence, certain that what they say to each other will not be revealed to anyone else without foreknowledge and consent.

Be prepared to deal with friends who want as much of your time as your new spouse claims.

It is not uncommon that individuals who are about to get married will have friendships with persons of the opposite gender that are purely social. These can be persons with whom they share a workspace on the job, with whom they have often eaten lunch, and with whom they might have spent time after work or on the weekend as part of a group of friends. These friendships might be longstanding relationships that reach back to college or even high school. There may have been a more intimate relationship at an earlier point in time, or there may never have been anything but a warm and wonderful friendship. But, now that a person is about to get married, he or she needs to put some boundaries around these friendships for the sake of his or her future spouse and marriage.

Opposite-gender friends may continue to call the house after the marriage, and that can become uncomfortable for the spouse who does not know this person as well or who does not like the idea of another man calling his wife (or another woman calling her husband) at home on a regular basis. Most mature people can understand and accept friendships that existed prior to their marriage, but they should be able to expect that those friendships will not consume as much time after the marriage as they did before the marriage. It is better if you put some limits on how much time you spend with those kinds of friends once you say I do. As innocent as it may seem at first, some friends have a way of intruding into the "one-flesh" relationship.

A former spouse can be a future problem, so be sure you
have clearly and definitively dissolved all previous
relationships before you get married.

As a result of the high rate of divorce followed by remarriage, there
are many couples who must contend with the presence of former
spouses as a part of their daily lives. This is most often the case when
custody for children from a former marriage is shared by both
partners, who want to have a continuing involvement in the lives of
their children no matter what has happened in the relationship with
their former spouse. As uncomfortable as this triangle can become for
all involved, there is little that can be done to prevent it except for a
stark reduction in the instances of divorce. Conflicts often arise when
visitation rights are disturbed or when patterns of parental discipline
vary between one of the birth parents and the new spouse of the
custodial parent. Patience and a little good humor can allow most
couples to endure these inconveniences.

The danger occurs when the former spouse appears to have a continuing claim on the time and attention of a person who is now married to
someone else. Premarital counseling sessions must deal candidly with this
problem, because it can be the undoing of a marriage. Many persons may
enter into a marital relationship having had a former spouse, but the
emphasis must always be on the word *former!* There must never come a
time when the present spouse must contend with a former spouse for the
time or attention of his or her new partner. Even worse, except when it
may relate to what is best for the children of a previous relationship, a
present spouse should never have to hear what the former spouse would
have done in any particular situation. I am not an advocate of divorce,
but I am quite clear about one thing: When a couple consents to
"forsaking all others," those words must also apply to the person(s) to
whom such words were spoken earlier in their lives.

Adultery has always been the most serious violation
of the principle of fidelity.

While it has been shown that the concept of fidelity is a far broader
topic than simply avoiding extramarital affairs, this traditional aspect
of the concept of fidelity must also be addressed. Nothing can kill a

marriage faster than sexual infidelity on the part of the husband or the wife. Marriage is a covenant, a partnership based on trust and confidence in each other. Even a single act of adultery can undermine that trust and confidence. I firmly believe that adultery can be *forgiven,* and I will argue that point in the next chapter dealing with forgiveness. What is more questionable is whether or not adultery will soon be *forgotten.*

Trust between a husband and a wife is an essential ingredient if a marriage is going to last. There will be many occasions when a couple will be apart for extended periods of time, sometimes measured in hours and often measured in days. There must be the confidence on the part of both spouses that prolonged absences are not simply opportunities for romantic flings with third parties. "Forsaking all others" must very definitely include the idea of remaining faithful to your spouse by avoiding any and all extramarital affairs.

Marriage is two people becoming one flesh.
In both Genesis 2:24 and Ephesians 5:31, marriage is envisioned as the union where "the two shall become one flesh." Implicit in this image is the wonder and mystery that surrounds marriage. Two people are joined together for life, and within that sacred union they share fully and equally in each other's joys and sorrows and hold their earthly possessions in common because they are perceived as being one.

When I served as a foreman of a grand jury panel in our county, we were briefed on the various crimes that would come before us for possible indictment. One of them was financial fraud, wherein a person would sign someone else's name to a check or to a credit-card receipt. However, we were told that no such charge would come before us when it involved a married couple, because in the eyes of the law those two persons are considered to be acting "as one" where financial transactions are involved.

What a wonderful thing it would be if every couple would understand this concept of acting "as one" and if they would let that image inform them in every area of their married life, and especially as it concerns this area of sexual fidelity.

The challenge for a long-term marriage is to be faithful unto death.

In Revelation 2:10 John is writing to the church in Smyrna that is apparently going through a period of persecution. Their faith in Jesus Christ is being severely tested, and John wants to offer them both a word of encouragement and a word of challenge. He says to them, "Be faithful, even to the point of death, and I will give you the crown of life." I believe these words can be appropriated and applied to our discussion of fidelity in marriage. If you want to enjoy a long, happy, and healthy marriage, then there are several things that you must do, and those include practicing fidelity in each of the forms I have outlined here. Be faithful to one another until death do you part and God will give you a healthy and happy marriage!

Questions for you to consider

1. How prepared are you to enter into a lifelong, monogamous relationship with your soon-to-be spouse?

2. Are there any former relationships you will need to be concerned about after you get married? If so, how will you handle them?

3. Can you think of any family or friends who might try to insert their opinions and advice into your marriage whether you request that advice or not? How will you respond to such attempts?

4. Are you committed to staying together in marriage for better or for worse? What actions or attitudes could have the effect of causing one of you to end the relationship?

5. Discuss the idea of marriage as being a "one-flesh" union. Are you prepared to embrace all that such a union represents?

6. What steps are necessary to safeguard against allowing your love for your children to obscure or replace your love for each other?

5
Forgiveness
How Many Times Shall I Forgive?

"Lord, how many times shall I forgive my brother when he
sins against me? Up to seven times?"
—Matthew 18:21

I DO NOT KNOW of a single married couple, whether they have
been married five months, five years, or are observing their fiftieth
wedding anniversary, that has not had to offer or accept forgiveness
from each other at some point along the way. Spouses are human and
we will make mistakes. Marriage involves two human beings who have
had different personalities, different life experiences, and different
goals and aspirations. Now those same two people are attempting to
live together for the rest of their lives, for better or for worse.

A willingness to forgive your spouse is essential
for a healthy marriage.
As in every other area of life, people who are married can say or do
the wrong things. As a result of that reality, feelings can be hurt and
the strongest of relationships can be strained. Over the course of time,
you and your spouse are going to have to learn to give and receive
forgiveness from each other. One of you is going to be late for dinner
or will neglect to call to say that you cannot keep an agreed upon
commitment. One of you is going to forget a birthday, Valentine's
Day, or some special sentimental date has come and gone (first
meeting, first date, first kiss, engagement, anniversary, etc.). These

things may seem small later in life, but for some couples such oversights in the early stages of their relationship can be heartbreaking. However, they can also become early occasions to practice forgiveness. If your marriage cannot withstand these small hurts in the early days of your new life together, your relationship may face real danger later on when far more serious hurts and disappointments may occur.

Marriage is a God-ordained institution where two people enter into a covenant relationship with each other. As we established in the previous chapter, at the center of that covenant are the words "for better or for worse, for richer or for poorer, in sickness and in health, for as long as we both shall live." The only way a covenant based on these words can last for any significant length of time is if both parties are willing to extend forgiveness to each other when something hurtful or offensive has taken place. If mistakes cannot be tolerated and if failures of any kind cannot be forgiven, then people should not get married in the first place, because if they cannot offer forgiveness to a spouse who has said or done something hurtful or offensive, then that marriage will not last very long.

A Christian's sense of forgiveness should be informed by the teachings of the Bible.

Forgiving our spouse should come more quickly to us as Christians because we understand that we ourselves have been forgiven for our sins by God, and in response to that gracious act, God expects that we will forgive one another. That is the basis of the parable in Matthew 18:23-35, in which one man is forgiven a huge debt that he owed, but then refuses to forgive a much smaller debt that was owed to him. The God who shows mercy and forgiveness to us fully expects that we will do the same toward one another. That same principle is spelled out in the words of the Lord's Prayer, which says, "Forgive us our debts, as we also have forgiven our debtors" (Matthew 6:12). Paul makes a similar point in Ephesians 4:32 when he says, "Be kind and compassionate to one another, forgiving each other, just as in Christ God forgave you." These words apply as much, if not more to our spouse than to any other relationship in which we are involved on the job, within the family, or in our various social settings.

Consider whether you know when it is time to forgive.
In the course of living together day in and day out, you and your spouse may do things that could be considered irritating or annoying, but the actions involved are not hurtful and do not rise to the level of requiring something as spiritually mature as extending forgiveness. In their book *Questions Couples Ask: Answers to the Top 100 Marital Questions*, Les and Leslie Parrott speak to the issue when they write:

> Forgiveness is not for feelings of annoyance. Nor is it for feelings of disappointment. Your spouse may not think to buy your favorite cereal on a trip to the grocery, but disappointment is not the same as betrayal, and you don't need to forgive disappointments.[1]

Annoyances, disappointments, and other mild irritations in marriage simply require a couple to be mature enough to overlook such trivialities.

What you and your spouse must do is be sensitive to those instances when something serious has been said or done that cannot be easily overlooked. That is the time when forgiveness must be extended if the relationship, which has already been affected by the offending act, is to continue to be loving and healthy. The Parrotts are helpful at this point as well. They note:

> Forgiveness is reserved for deep feelings of hurt. When you feel that your partner has intentionally wounded you or been unfair, it is time for forgiveness. In fact, the best indicator we know of for determining when it is time to forgive is when you feel like getting even. Forgiveness releases us from the pain of the past by surrendering our desire to make our spouse suffer too.[2]

Extending forgiveness to your spouse who has said or done something that hurt you or that you consider unfair should not be thought of as optional. A healthy marriage requires that a couple be willing and able to forgive each other when confronted with offenses far more serious than everyday irritations and annoyances.

"Don't lie to me. . . . "

One of the cornerstones of a healthy marriage is honesty between husband and wife. You do not always have to agree with each other, but you had better tell the truth to each other the first time a question is asked and every time thereafter. One single instance of not telling the truth can harm your marriage, and a pattern of lies and half-truths can undermine a marital relationship altogether. Neither of you should have to wonder whether or not the other is telling the truth. However, if one of you does lie or speak a half-truth to the other, the question becomes whether or not lying can be forgiven.

Lying and half-truths are not the same as the charade you may employ to keep your spouse from learning about a surprise party you are planning for an upcoming birthday. It is not the same as pretending not to notice when your partner has "put on a pound or two." But when a direct question about family finances, job security, or some health issue is raised, it is once again time to be absolutely candid and frank. The one thing couples have repeatedly told me during our premarital counseling sessions is that they want and expect a spouse to always tell them the truth. The phrase that is most often used at this point in premarital counseling sessions is direct and straight to the point: "Don't lie to me!"

The challenge for every couple who expect and demand honesty in their relationship is whether or not they can forgive the spouse who has not been honest. Perhaps the truth will not be told for what the dishonest person thinks is a good reason. Maybe one of you will not want the other to worry about something. Maybe your partner will say or do something embarrassing outside of the home that he or she wants to keep from coming to your attention. Maybe pride and vanity will get in the way and you will speak a half-truth in order to protect your own ego. Whatever the circumstances may become, you need to consider now whether or not you will be willing to forgive each other should something like this take place within your marriage.

Lying and deception can undermine your marriage.

Whatever the reason, the fact is that when you lie to your spouse you undermine your marriage. Telling the truth in all situations is always important, but the consequences of not doing it are more severe when you are newlyweds because you are just beginning to establish the foundation of what you hope will be a lifelong union. If you have to wonder whether or not you can trust your spouse, there will be cracks in your foundation that could eventually cause the marriage to collapse.

It is at those times that forgiveness must be extended. Of course, whichever one of you is not honest will need to apologize and work at being honest and telling the truth from that point on. However, what happens next in your marriage will remain ultimately in the hands of whichever one of you is lied to by the other. If you are that person, it would be fair for you to tell your spouse how much this incident has hurt you, and that you expect that it will not happen again—and if you are the person who is lying, your spouse will have the right to say the same to you. Of course, it would be a good idea for those words of rebuke to be spoken in the spirit of Ephesians 4:15, which exhorts us always to speak "the truth in love."

The question remains, What happens after the words of rebuke have been spoken and the feelings of hurt or offense have been expressed? This is where you have to ask yourself the question, Can I forgive my spouse for lying to me? Whether it was done intentionally or accidentally, you will find yourself having to confront this question over the course of your marriage. It is important that both of you think clearly about this subject, and it is just as important for you to realize that at one time or another each of you may stand in need of forgiveness from the other for not having been completely honest and candid.

"But you promised..."

One of the joys of married life is having a friend and partner upon whom you can depend. Over the course of any given day there will be more things that need to be accomplished than either of you can or should be expected to do alone. One of you may ask the other to ease the burden by agreeing to assume responsibility for one of the things that needs to be done. It may be picking up items from the grocery store, paying a bill on the way home, carrying out the trash before the garbage truck arrives in your neighborhood, or depositing money in the checking account. Whatever the task is, from the moment that you agree to do it, your spouse has every reason to believe that it is going to be done. After all, you promised....

Now comes the end of that day and the grocery items needed for dinner were not purchased, the trash is still sitting in the house, the bills have not been paid, and the deposit to cover those bills already mailed has not been made. You had promised to do it, but you got distracted and forgot about the tasks you had agreed to do. It was not your intention to make a promise to your spouse that would take some of the load off his or her shoulders and then not keep that promise. It was just one of those days. This is a moment when irritation and disappointment can intrude into your marriage, and what happens next depends upon how well you or your spouse can exercise the art of forgiveness.

When a promise is not kept, especially as it involves keeping the household running smoothly, a door is opened up for blame and accusations of not caring about the other person or of being unreliable. Couples need to be careful here, because often it will not only be the immediate issue at hand that will be discussed, but past instances of promises made but not kept as well. Again, a large part of being married is the joy and confidence that comes from knowing that you have someone working with you toward a common end. Part of the stress and strain of marriage comes when something does not get done and one person says to the other, "But you promised...."

Forgive your spouse as you will later want to be forgiven.

While the one who made the promise needs to apologize for not having done what he or she promised to do, that moment of disappointment can be turned into a time of spiritual growth and renewal for both of you when the person who might consider assigning blame decides instead to offer forgiveness. Let the words of Paul in Colossians 3:13 inform you at that moment: "Bear with each other and forgive whatever grievances you may have against one another. Forgive as the Lord forgave you." This is always good advice for you when your spouse makes a promise to you but is unable to keep it for whatever the reason. That is because eventually the roles will be reversed, and you will welcome having a spirit of forgiveness displayed toward you when your spouse turns to you and says, "But you promised...."

Consider what you will do when problems persist.

What makes forgiveness a complicated thing is that the very behavior we may be willing to forgive if it only occurs once has a tendency to continue to recur. We are therefore forced to ask ourselves the question of Matthew 18:21: "How many times shall I forgive?" The underlying assumption in the question (and in Jesus' response in the subsequent parable) is that problematic behavior has a way of persisting long after it has been first forgiven. The question then becomes, Do I keep on forgiving behaviors and attitudes that my spouse knows I dislike, but that my spouse continues to exhibit? Jesus tells us to forgive the same sin committed by our loved one not just seven times, but seventy times seven. This principle *must* apply if a couple is to enjoy a healthy and happy marriage.

The things that require recurring forgiveness may involve any of the issues already discussed above or in previous chapters of this book: issues of housekeeping, financial management, tone of voice or facial expressions, quick-tempered remarks, failure to follow through on agreed-upon responsibilities, or spending too much time away from home, whether at work or with other friends. Or, the problem areas may be unique to a particular married couple and thus may not be mentioned specifically anywhere in this study.

The question is the same whatever the case: How many times will I forgive my spouse when he or she continues to practice this behavior? And the answer is clear: We must be willing to forgive each other over and over again because that is exactly what God does toward us. Unless we want God to forgive our sins only once and then hold them against us thereafter, we need to practice the principle of regular and repeated forgiveness in the context of our marriage.

By the time people get married, their personalities have been pretty well established, and sudden and drastic changes in behavior in most areas of life are unlikely. People who are sloppy housekeepers today will probably be sloppy housekeepers tomorrow and next week and next year. What will one person say or do when, after forgiving a spouse once for this behavior, the problem continues? People who tend to overspend as a result of impulse on one occasion can be expected to engage in impulse shopping many times in the future. Having forgiven an impulsive spouse once for upsetting the family budget, what will the other partner do when that behavior presents itself again and again into the future?

The one thing that keeps most marriages from sinking into resentment and hostility, or even deteriorating into separation and eventual divorce, is the understanding that forgiveness within marriage cannot be viewed as a one-time gesture. You will quite often have to be willing to forgive your spouse for the same behavior or attitude on more than one occasion. I am asking you to personalize the question that Peter asked of Jesus, "How many times shall I forgive?"

"Forgive each other every day from the bottom of your hearts."

One of the most moving and instructive statements about forgiveness in marriage that I have ever encountered comes from Dietrich Bonhoeffer, the German pastor and theologian who was killed by the Nazis on April 9, 1945. For two years prior to his death, Bonhoeffer carried on a pastoral ministry from his prison cell. One of the ways he did this was through the letters he wrote to friends and family on the outside. One of those letters, written in May of 1943, was directed to a couple that had only recently been married. It is clear from the tone of the letter that Bonhoeffer knew this couple very well and had wanted to be present at their wedding, but a letter was all that could be done. In that letter, now known as "A Wedding Sermon from a Prison Cell," Bonhoeffer wrote these words about forgiveness:

> Live together in the forgiveness of your sins, for without it no human fellowship, least of all marriage, can survive. Don't insist on your rights, don't blame each other, don't judge or condemn each other, don't find fault with each other, but accept each other as you are, and forgive each other every day from the bottom of your hearts.[3]

When you are able to "forgive each other every day from the bottom of your hearts," your marriage is most likely to thrive for the rest of your lives.

Do not take forgiveness from your spouse for granted.
While I am urging you to be willing to forgive each other over and over again, I will also state that you owe it to your spouse to make a good-faith effort to change or at least to try to control whatever behaviors or attitudes your spouse finds hurtful or offensive. You should not take for granted your spouse's willingness to forgive by continuing to do what you know he or she doesn't like, and then assuring yourself that he or she will forgive you no matter what you do. In Romans 6:1-2, Paul said, "Shall we go on sinning so that grace may increase? By no means!" Just as Christians should not take for granted the grace that flows from the heart of God, so one spouse should not take for granted nor knowingly abuse the forgiveness that flows from the love of his or her marriage partner.

Simply stated, while forgiveness may need to be extended on a regular basis by one person, the other person should seek to behave in ways that make such regular need for forgiveness no longer necessary. There are very few behaviors that cannot be altered if you have the right motivation. People have kicked addictions to chemical substances because they wanted to get on with their lives free from crime and the criminal justice system. People have altered their eating habits and lost weight because they wanted to preserve their health and extend their lives. Others have quit smoking cigarettes for the same reason. Surely we should be willing to work just as hard to alter whatever behaviors we have engaged in that have hurt or offended our spouse—for the health of our marriages.

After all, the person who is expressing injury over our behaviors is our spouse, our "one-flesh" partner for life. Part of the language of the marriage vow says that you will "love, honor, and cherish" each other. One of the best ways to keep that part of your vows is to work as hard as you can to give up those actions and attitudes that have been hurtful or offensive to your spouse. When spouses are working both to show forgiveness when offended *and* to reduce and remove the actions that created the initial offense, that couple is laying a solid foundation for a healthy marriage.

Forgiveness will be needed from the moment you say I do.
It is safe to say that the need to work on extending forgiveness and on

removing things that your spouse considers offensive will begin almost as soon as your wedding ceremony concludes. No matter how long the courtship may have lasted, marriage creates an entirely new relationship between the husband and the wife. Each person brings a set of assumptions and expectations about how things are supposed to happen in marriage. When those assumptions and expectations are not met, a chill can fall over the relationship that only a spirit of forgiveness can thaw.

These assumptions may involve the roles that each person is supposed to play within the household, ranging from paying the bills to emptying the garbage to being a passionate lover night after night. They can involve other patterns of behavior, such as attending church together every Sunday or making multiple phone calls throughout the day just to say "I love you." Expectations can also involve an individual having a certain time and space in which to experience a certain amount of privacy where even the spouse does not intrude. All of these assumptions, when they do not come to pass as hoped and expected, can become opportunities for disappointment and hurt. On the other hand, each of these disappointments can also become an opportunity to practice forgiveness.

The longer you wait the harder it will become to forgive.

The last thing that needs to be said about forgiveness is best stated in Ephesians 4:26 which says, " 'In your anger do not sin': Do not let the sun go down while you are still angry." Newly married couples often allow hours and even days to go by while they sulk over something that one spouse has said or done, or not said or done, to or for the other spouse. Something has disappointed them that they have not yet learned how to process in the context of their expectations about married life. As a result, they do exactly the wrong thing, which is to *stop talking to each other.*

This dynamic is what is known as conflict avoidance (which was introduced in the chapter about frankness). It takes one of several forms, all of which can be damaging to your marriage. Authors Les and Leslie Parrott are helpful once again when they discuss some of the forms of conflict avoidance.

Some people deal with potential conflict by simply avoiding issues about which they disagree. They might postpone discussion about a problem to a later time, or they might simply ignore it altogether. Some couples deny that a problem exists at all. Still other couples are prone to withdraw from conflict by shutting down or actually leaving.[4]

The Parrotts end their discussion about conflict avoidance with a clear and direct warning that you need to take seriously: "Not being willing to voice one's frustrations to a spouse can be like a toxin to a marriage. If the avoidance is not corrected, it is a definite sign of danger."[5]

The biblical principle found in Ephesians 4:26 is instructive in two ways. First, it is not unusual that something you or your spouse say or do can result in feelings of anger, pain, or betrayal. We expect more from our closest loved ones in terms of support, thoughtfulness, patience, compassion, and understanding. Thus, when our loved ones do not display these qualities or when they hurt or disappoint us in some other way, it can cause a deeper anger and resentment than would be the case if the same offense were committed by someone less central to our lives. Moments of anger do not mean that you and your spouse no longer love each other. Nor do such moments mean that your marriage is in danger. However, you need to address the causes of that anger sooner rather than later.

While Ephesians says, "Do not let the sun go down on your anger," it may not always be possible to address the problem or work things out to the point that apologies can be offered and forgiveness extended on the same day when the triggering event took place. It may be that after a cooling-off period of a few hours the situation will have calmed down and life can go on as normal. That is usually the case with things that are aggravations. However, when something has occurred in your marriage that has been genuinely hurtful or disappointing to you or your spouse, you need to address that issue as soon as possible.

Many couples consider adultery to be the unforgivable marital sin. In most of the premarital counseling sessions that I have done, there is only one thing that most couples seem determined to hold on to as being unforgivable, and that is adultery. As mentioned in the chapter on fidelity, infidelity may take many other forms, and those other forms will also require forgiveness. But sexual infidelity will never become an issue for many couples. I hope and pray that this will be the case with you. Such couples work hard to keep any third party from sharing in the intimacy that they reserve only for each other. I have been married for twenty-seven years, and adultery has never once intruded into our relationship.

Unfortunately this is not the case in every marriage. Some people even maintain sexual relationships with other persons during the courtship. In many instances they maintain those extramarital relationships and carry on additional liaisons after they have consented to the words "forsaking all others" as well. Adultery is a hateful thing that can place strains on what to all appearances are the strongest and healthiest of marriages. The question that you must consider is whether or not adultery is to be viewed as the one act for which you could not forgive your spouse should it occur.

There is only one unforgivable sin in the Bible.

I agree that adultery is an awful sin that grieves the Holy Spirit as much as it hurts and offends the wronged spouse. It is a violation not only of the words of the wedding vows, but of the "one-flesh" principle that is the foundation upon which marriage is established. Having said that, the question must still be asked whether adultery should be allowed to stand as an unpardonable sin. In Mark 3:28-29, Jesus stated that God is willing to forgive all of our sins, except the sin of blasphemy against the Holy Spirit. This passage raises the bar of forgiveness awfully high and forces us to reconsider the question of whether or not even something as hurtful and humiliating as adultery can and should be forgiven.

Let's learn about love from Hosea and Gomer.

One of the most shocking and revealing stories about the love of God toward us is found in the Book of Hosea where that prophet is told to marry a prostitute named Gomer. Over and over again Gomer not only commits adultery, but gives birth to children that are the living proof of her unfaithfulness. Surely Hosea had grounds to sue for divorce and end that marriage. Of course, that story is something of an Old Testament parable, in which Hosea represents God and Gomer represents the people of God—both in ancient Israel and in the Body of Christ today.

We have been unfaithful to God, investing our lives and our faith in many other people and places. Despite our spiritual adultery, we hear the words of God found in Hosea 11:8, where a loving and forgiving God says to a faithless people, "How can I give you up, Ephraim? … My heart is changed within me; all my compassion is aroused." This is God's way of dealing with us, and it is meant to be the model by which we then deal with one another. God shows boundless love toward us by forgiving our sins of unfaithfulness, and in return for that God expects that we will forgive each other when an act of unfaithfulness intrudes into our human relationships.

This moment may never come in your marriage, but if it does, nobody expects that forgiveness will be easy to offer. Nevertheless, forgiveness *is* the message of Scripture, from the Old Testament through the New Testament, and from Hosea and Gomer to Jesus, whose first words from the cross were "Father, forgive them, for they do not know what they are doing" (Luke 23:34). Those who take their vows "in the presence of God" must first of all live in such a way as to never require being forgiven of adultery. But, second, they must be ready and willing to offer forgiveness when deep hurt and a sense of betrayal threaten their marriage. No matter what the offense may have been, the willingness to express forgiveness is absolutely essential to the maintenance of a healthy, long-term marriage.

Don't wait too long to say I'm sorry.
No discussion of forgiveness would be complete without a stern reminder that forgiveness comes most quickly and works best in tandem with a sincere apology from whichever one of you caused the hurt. Acknowledging our sins and the hurts we have caused others has biblical roots just as deep as the call to extend forgiveness. In 1 John 1:9 we are told, "If we confess our sins, he is faithful and just and will forgive us our sins and purify us from all unrighteousness."

The same principle can and should apply in your marriage. When you are willing to acknowledge and apologize for those words and deeds that have hurt your spouse, you can expect to receive his or her forgiveness far more quickly than if you either stall or refuse to do so. One of you needs to apologize and one of you needs to be ready to forgive. The sooner you can do that, the sooner you and your spouse will be back on the road to "happily ever after."

Questions for you to consider

1. Is there anything your spouse could do that you would not be able to forgive? Share that information with your intended partner.

2. Have you already had to deal with forgiving one another even prior to getting married? If so, what happened between you and how did you resolve that issue?

3. Can you forgive things as soon as you have received an apology, or do you tend to hold on to hurt feelings for days and even weeks? What about your intended spouse?

4. How do you respond to being hurt—with a hot temper and angry words? With silence and a cold shoulder? Or, are you able to speak the truth in love?

5. What would you do if the behavior you have already forgiven once continues to occur?

6. Are either of you easily hurt or offended by things that might be said or done by your spouse? If so, in what areas is that most likely to happen?

7. In what ways does your faith as a Christian inform your understanding of the role of forgiveness in life in general and in marriage in particular?

6

Finances

Money Management—
A Key to a Successful Marriage

She watches over the affairs of her household and does not
eat the bread of idleness.
—Proverbs 31:27

THE BEATLES HAD A SONG that said, "Money can't buy me love."
Let me suggest to you that all the love in the world may not be enough
to sustain your marriage if you and your spouse are always arguing
over money. I do not question for a moment the central role that love
must play in your relationship, but love alone will not pay your bills
or keep a roof over your heads or put food on your table several times
a day. In fact, love has a way of blocking out a variety of important
details that contribute to the success or failure of our marriages. Before
you say I do, be sure that both of you have come to some mutual
agreement on how to handle the family finances. Having such a
discussion is something you should not omit no matter how much
you love one another. The issue is not so much a matter of how much
or how little money with which you may have to work. The crucial
issue, especially at the beginning of your marriage, is coming to a
common understanding about how the family finances will be managed.

In his book *Debt-Free Living*, Christian financial advisor Larry
Burkett makes the observation that "80% of young couples that get a
divorce by age thirty report that financial problems were a primary
cause of the divorce."[1] A long-term, successful marriage requires that

you and your spouse have a clear understanding of each other's past financial handicaps, your present financial habits, and your future financial hopes.

Begin your financial planning by calculating how much each of you already owes.

The first issue that must be addressed prior to marriage is the level of debt each of you is bringing to the relationship. It is unfair to hide this information from each other, primarily because it will be impossible to hide it from future lenders when you seek a mortgage, consumer credit, or any other type of loan. Do not wait until you are turned down for a loan because of bad or overextended credit to tell your spouse the truth about your financial past. When you two become "one flesh," that oneness will quickly extend to include the debt you are bringing with you into the marriage. Be sure that you know just how much combined debt you will be facing.

As couples delay marriage into their late twenties and early thirties, and especially as persons consider remarriage once they are in their forties and fifties, there is likely to be an extensive financial history that each partner brings to the marriage. There may be extensive credit-card debt or unpaid college and graduate-school loans. There may be unsettled tax liens or a history of delinquent rent or mortgage payments. It is not uncommon even for persons in their late teens to carry several credit cards. The chances of being overextended by the time you are ready to get married are far more likely now than they have ever been in the history of this country.

Be frank about your financial situation, even if you have to reveal problems from the past.

Remember the earlier chapter about frankness; be sure you are completely honest with each other about your past financial dealings. Are there any attachments to your (or your intended spouse's) paycheck? Have you ever been through a bankruptcy? Are there any unpaid medical or dental expenses, any court-ordered child-support payments, or any outstanding loans from a financial institution or friend that must be paid off? You cannot climb the mountain to future financial security until you both clearly understand how deep is the valley of debt and bad credit in which your marriage is beginning.

Just as I have urged you to be honest about your sexual history, it is equally important that you be frank and thorough in a discussion of your financial history. In both instances, things you do not discuss honestly at the outset of your marriage can, and probably will, come back to haunt you later in your relationship. The older both of you are, the more thorough this discussion needs to be because both of you will have had a lot of experience at handling or mishandling money. When it comes to a premarital discussion about financial history, advice from your neighborhood swimming pool is helpful: Look before you leap!

Discuss your individual views about spending and saving before marriage.

Spendthrift vs. Scrooge. Once you and your spouse have had a discussion about your financial histories, it is time to talk with equal candor about the financial habits each of you is practicing at the present time. Once again, it is not being suggested that you are going to have to mirror the behavior of the other every step of the way. What is being sought in this discussion is awareness, not necessarily agreement.

Does one of you spend money as quickly as you earn it, while the other one prefers to save as much as possible, both for a rainy day and for a brighter future? If you believe strongly in using cash for all expenses except, perhaps, the mortgage, a car payment, and your honeymoon, then imagine the conflicts that can arise if your spouse has a tendency to charge even the smallest of expenses, run several credit cards up to their limit, and then use layaway for what you cannot afford to carry away from the store that day.

Sears vs. Saks Fifth Ave. We live in a culture that seems to espouse two widely different values so far as shopping for clothing and other consumer goods are concerned: top of the line versus the bargain basement. Some people will purchase nothing that does not come from the most expensive store and that does not carry the label of some *chic* fashion designer. Other people find such behavior wasteful and prefer to shop for sale items at discount stores. Many of the shopping malls that dot the American landscape offer shoppers plenty of choices so far as luxury goods versus low prices are concerned. Will you and your spouse be shopping together in the same stores, or will you agree to meet each other somewhere in the mall after each of you has gone off in a separate direction?

As I tell couples in my premarital counseling sessions, it does not matter at all to me what your respective shopping habits are. What does matter to me, and what should matter to you, is that you and your spouse know each other's habits and preferences in this regard. More importantly, I urge you to approach this issue with one of two long-term options in mind. First, you can agree to accommodate each other and work out an approach to buying clothes and other consumer goods that is mutually agreeable. Second, you can agree to disagree in this area and continue to shop and spend according to your particular tastes and desires. What I hope you will *not* do is let every trip to the mall or to the market become another occasion for a fight about family finances. Take seriously the observation of Larry Burkett that was mentioned earlier: Arguments about money, not the act of adultery, are more likely to cause your marriage to end in divorce court.

Discuss the importance of who should be the primary wage earner in your marriage.

With increasing frequency I am discovering that the future wife earns considerably more in salary than her future husband. You and your spouse may view being a two-income family as beneficial in that it allows you to reach financial security more quickly. But both of you need to be honest about your feelings should the woman have a higher income than the man. Some men may actually feel threatened by that fact, inheriting from our society the cultural assumption that the husband should be the primary "breadwinner," with any income earned by the wife being considered supplemental. By the same token, some wives may resist any notion of the husband being the "head of the house" when it is their income that makes the largest contribution to the family finances.

How do the two of you feel about the wife earning more than the husband? Many couples no longer use such concepts as "head of the house" or any other image that implies male headship. They view themselves as partners in every way, and the fact that the female partner provides the primary financial support for their home is inconsequential. However, some men feel their very manhood is threatened by wives who earn more than they do, and that fact can create problems for the relationship that may last as long as the income disparity continues.

In an article in *Essence* magazine entitled "18 Months That Saved Our Marriage," this issue was confronted by a couple going through premarital counseling where the woman earned five times more than her future husband. The issue of income disparity affected both persons though in quite different ways. The woman was concerned by how little her future husband was "bringing to the table." The man was intimidated and "embarrassed" by the fact that his future wife was doing so much better financially than he was. They both acknow-ledged that it was important for them to have addressed this issue before they got married, because "discussing their financial disparities up front helped defuse a potentially explosive issue that could have caused major problems in their marriage."[2]

If such an income disparity exists in your relationship, you need to be informed by the conclusion finally reached by the man discussed in the *Essence* story. He said, "The classes [premarital] helped me understand that marriage isn't about who makes the most money, but about understanding where each person is coming from, and trying to get someplace higher together."[3] This was not his position before the premarital counseling, and I would suspect that his initial discom-fort with this income disparity is reflective of the views of a great many men. Make this issue one of the topics of conversation when you and your future spouse start talking about finances.

It is never too early to start planning ahead for the stages of life that are coming sooner or later.

In *Alice in Wonderland* by Lewis Carroll, this bit of wisdom can be found: "If you don't know where you are going then any road can get you there." That advice has implications for the kind of financial planning you should bring into your marriage. You need to decide where you want to go in order to chart the course that can get you moving in that direction. Talk with your spouse about any long-term financial goals he or she might have, and be equally open about what hopes and dreams you have where finances are concerned. The sooner you start talking about it, the sooner you can start walking down the road to making your dreams come true.

There are five standard areas of financial planning you should discuss before you say I do. Once you know each other's views on these crucial issues, you can begin working as a team to accomplish each goal within an agreed upon timetable. The five areas are home ownership, childcare and education, retirement planning, debt-free living, and healthcare and life insurance coverage for both of you. Each of these deserves some brief discussion.

Home ownership. Home ownership continues to be the foundation of the American Dream of financial security. Money spent on rent builds up wealth for whoever owns the place you are renting. Money spent on a mortgage builds up equity in your name and allows you to leverage your overall finances with much more flexibility. Do you and your spouse both want to own a home? Many couples who get married these days have already crossed this bridge with one or both of them living in their own home. If that is not the case with you, then find out how important this is to each of you and start moving in that direction.

It will require some sacrifices in order to accumulate the 10 to 35 percent down payment that many banks and mortgage companies charge for your first home. It will also require a "squeaky clean" credit report. Who is going to loan you $100,000 to $200,000 to buy a house when you have not made prompt payments on a $1,000 big screen television or a $2,000 cruise through the Caribbean? However, if a home of your own is a dream that you and your intended spouse share, then both of you need to commit to whatever financial plan you think will get you where you want to go.

Childcare and education. If and when children become a part of your family, you will need to consider how you will cover the estimated $180,000 required to meet the various expenses of a single child for the first eighteen years of its life—costs that encompass food, clothing, and childcare. Beyond that, you must consider the fact that without some type of formal education beyond high school, that child's future success in life may be greatly limited. Not every child may need or want to attend a four-year college, but the cost of attending a community college or some certified, technical, or vocational program should be anticipated. The average cost of four years of tuition, room and board, books, and other fees at a public university in the state where you live has already exceeded $50,000. If you or your child expect to attend one of the nation's private colleges or universities, that amount can easily be doubled. You can do the math if you and your spouse plan to have more than one child.

Having children is not just a biological or legal issue concerning whether you and your spouse are able to conceive or adopt a child. Having children is not only a moral and theological issue where birth control and abortion questions are concerned—although I strongly urge you to be on the same page where those issues are concerned. Having children is a decision that has profound financial implications for your family. You may not start working on this aspect of parenthood until you are embracing your first child, but here again, the sooner you start saving and planning for your child's future, the better off you will be.

Retirement planning. Two things seem to be readily apparent when you consider your long-term financial needs. The first is that people are living longer after they have retired from their jobs, and the second is that Social Security, if it is even around when you reach retirement age, will not come close to meeting your financial needs once your salaried income has come to an end. You will have to plan for your financial needs after you reach retirement age, and the time to start preparing for the eventuality is *now!*

You and your intended spouse will need to consider which approaches you are most comfortable using, but several strategies can help you get where you are trying to go. Despite the occasional roller coaster rides of the Dow Jones Industrial Average, the stock market remains a reliable way to plan for long-term financial needs. The younger you are when you start investing, the greater the return you can expect from the stock market. If you do not trust yourself when it comes to selecting stocks, choose several reliable mutual funds.

Socially conscious investors can find mutual funds that avoid companies that deal in such products as tobacco, alcohol, gambling casinos,
or weapons and military contracts.

Government bonds and U.S. savings bonds are also ways to pursue
an investment strategy that can produce long-term growth without
accepting as much risk. Certificates of deposit (CDs), money market
funds, passbook savings accounts, and interest-bearing checking accounts are low-risk/low-return approaches to saving, but they beat
doing nothing at all, which is what most Americans have been doing
for the last forty years.

Company pension funds may have been reliable when your parents
were in the workforce, but they are a lot less secure today with
companies going bankrupt, being plundered or bought out by corporate raiders who want to increase profits by reducing costs—beginning
with amounts being paid into pension funds. Be sure that you and
your future spouse understand the importance of keeping an eye not
only on the house in which you want to live tomorrow, but on how
and where you plan to live when you are retired. How you will be able
to live then increasingly depends on the plans you make now.

Debt-free living. This may or may not be an important issue for
either one of you, but you owe it to yourself to have this conversation.
Imagine what life could be like if your lives were not swamped in debt,
especially credit card debt. If your income is sufficient to support all
the debt you have, and if you do not mind paying more in interest on
your debt than you are earning on your savings and investments, then
move on to the next topic. But before you do, consider the words of
Proverbs 22:7, which says, "The rich rule over the poor, and the
borrower is servant to the lender." Consider also the words of Paul in
Romans 13:8: "Let no debt remain outstanding, except the continuing
debt to love one another."

It is extremely important that you and your spouse be clear about
your respective views concerning living with excessive debt. Like
everything else being discussed in this section, achieving debt-free
living requires time and discipline. So, if one of you is pulling in that
direction while the other one is pulling in an opposite direction, you
will be placing a strain on your "one-flesh" relationship. Whether you

already agree with each other, agree to accommodate each other in some way, or simply agree to disagree, this is another discussion you need to have before you say I do.

Health insurance. At a time when one medical procedure can result in financial ruin for persons who have no medical insurance, and at a time when more than 40 million Americans have no medical insurance and another 40 million have only limited health coverage, it is obvious that couples contemplating marriage need to know where they stand on this important topic. Will one or both of you have health insurance coverage for your family? Will that coverage include catastrophic care in the event of the need for some major surgery such as a transplant? Will that coverage include prescription drugs as well as dental and vision needs? Does it have disability coverage in case one or both of you are unable to work for any extended period of time?

If neither of you has health insurance coverage, then you need to think about what you will do if one of you should need extended medical care or rehabilitation. Sadly, this is a question that one out of every six Americans has to consider every day. It seems that our national leaders have no answer for this problem, and so it is up to each one of us to anticipate this need and figure out what we will do if and when the time comes.

Life insurance. Life insurance is another protection to consider for your family, and it is substantially more affordable than health coverage. Consult with a licensed professional for the coverage that is best for you at this point in your life, and remember that you can always increase or reduce the amount of coverage you have as your needs and goals in life change. The rule of thumb is that the amount of your coverage ought to be enough to match the income of the primary wage earner for a period of ten years so that the surviving family can maintain their present lifestyle for that period of time. At the very least, plan on an amount of life insurance that will cover all funeral expenses and the settling of any outstanding debts.

It may seem premature to discuss this topic, but I assure you based upon my experience as a pastor that death has made no promise to take our loved ones only after they have grown old. I once officiated at the wedding of a couple in June and presided at the funeral of the groom just a few months later. I have agonized with young widows left with children, a blizzard of bills, and a paralyzing grief that could have been at least partially abated if a simple life insurance policy had been in place that could have helped them keep the household together. These preparations are easy to make, and there is no good excuse for not doing so. Money can't buy love, but even a small amount of money well directed can buy a lot of peace of mind for you and your family "for as long as you both shall live" and even after "death do us part."

Other plans to be considered. While the items listed above are the most urgent financial plans to be discussed, there are a few other things I want to mention here for your eventual consideration. If you have a home mortgage, you may want to get mortgage insurance in case disability or death strikes the primary wage earner. You will want to keep an updated and notarized last will and testament in a place where your loved ones can find it. You should think about a living will in the event that you find yourself in a critical-care situation and you cannot speak for yourself on the matter of life support or organ transplants or donations. Consult a lawyer about granting durable power of attorney to each other, which involves a notarized document that allows you to sign legal documents in each other's stead should illness, injury, or even extended absence make it impossible for both of you to be present in person. Finally, more and more people are spending their final years in a nursing facility of one level of quality or another. By planning early for your long-term-care needs, you can approach this possibility with less anxiety. Here again, the expertise of a financial planner, insurance agent, or a trusted friend or family member can help get you started in each of these areas.

Discuss whether you will include tithing as part of your financial plan.

One of the financial decisions that every Christian has to make involves the level of church support you intend to build into your family budget. The biblical method of stewardship is tithing, or giving 10 percent of your household income to support the work of your church. You may want to give at a level that is higher than 10 percent, but most people find it a challenge just to reach that amount. Whether you choose to tithe based upon the gross or the net amount of your income (before or after taxes) is a matter you need to decide for yourself. I have always tithed off of my net amount since the gross amount involves tax deductions over which I have no control. In either case, you and your spouse need to discuss the issue of tithing as part of your financial strategy.

One way to think about financial planning that includes both tithing and savings is to use what is called the 10-10-80 plan of money management. In this approach you pay God first (a 10 percent tithe), you pay yourself second (putting another 10 percent of your income into a savings or investment instrument), and you pay your bills and other living expenses on the remaining 80 percent of your monthly income. It may take you a while to get into the habit or to establish the discipline of following this plan, but it is a sound approach to money management.

Someone once said that most people did not follow a plan that failed; most people simply failed to plan. The time to start planning for all of these areas of financial concern is sooner rather than later.

Discuss whether a married couple should have two separate bank accounts.

The decision to have you and your one-flesh partner share a joint checking account or maintain two separate accounts is both symbolically and substantively important. When both of you have been working prior to your marriage and when both of you have become accustomed to handling your own personal finances, it will require some adjustments to shift everything into one joint account. Should you decide to share a joint account, you will have to keep a more careful eye on your bank balance since you cannot be sure of what checks each of you has written or what cash withdrawals each of you has made on any given day. This is one of those decisions that has to be made rather soon since you will need to decide how to deposit your various sources of income and how to start paying the bills that will start coming in almost immediately after your wedding day.

Obviously the idea of pooling your financial resources into a joint banking account adds another dimension to the idea of the two of you becoming "one flesh." It gives strength to the notion that you are sharing everything together. His-and-her towels may work well in your bathroom, but the value of his-and-her checking accounts is something you will want to consider very carefully. Pronouns carry great meaning as they help to identify ownership and possession. What things are yours and what things belong to your spouse? This question does not pertain to such things as clothing or jewelry or personal care items. But when it comes to what is in the refrigerator, the pantry, the candy dish, or the checking account you might want to consider that *ours* is the best pronoun of all.

Discuss now which one of you is actually going to pay the bills.

The decision to work from a joint account does not resolve the question of precisely how the bills will get paid each month and how the savings and investment deposits will be made. Will one of you assume the responsibility for that part of running the household? Will you consult each month on how much is being spent and whether or not your expenses are exceeding your income? There has to be some order and routine so far as this area is concerned.

Some couples designate the wife to fulfill this role, especially if she happens not to work outside the home. Some husbands will insist on doing this as part of their understanding of being "head of the house." If both of you work outside the home and bring in a paycheck that supports your household, you can both make a claim on this responsibility. Just try to make this decision on the basis of something other than power.

Perhaps one of you is more attentive to detail and can keep better track of household expenses and incoming bills. Perhaps one of you works hours that are so hectic that you know it would be a bad idea for you to take on this task. Bills will start rolling in before your wedding photographs have been developed and returned. Whether you flip a coin, draw straws, or one of you simply concedes to the other, be sure that both of you know whose responsibility this is going to be. Whoever accepts this assignment must then review the chapter on fidelity and the importance of the words "but you promised...."

Give some consideration to the ethical question of where your money comes from.

There are any number of ways by which extra income can be brought into your home, but you and your spouse need to be clear about what things are or are not acceptable. One of you may have strong feelings about working on the Lord's Day and thus you would rather do without extra money than earn it by working on Sunday (or whatever your Sabbath might be). Some people approach casino gambling, horse racing, and state lotteries as an opportunity to "strike it rich." If you or your spouse view these actions as wasteful and perhaps even as morally questionable, then you need to make those views known and seek to honor each other on this point.

It is possible that someone may approach one of you about investing in a store that will sell beer, wine, and other varieties of alcohol along with lottery tickets. You may not be buying them, but you may have strong feelings about feeding and supporting the addictions with which others are affected. At least all these things are products that can be purchased and used legally. There are thousands of households across this country that bring in a little extra income by playing some small role in the distribution and sale of illegal drugs and through other illicit activities as well. It is most improbable that you or your spouse would ever engage in such activity, but compare notes with each other on this issue just to be sure.

Discuss whether either of you is interested in a prenuptial agreement.

Part of any thorough financial discussion must involve addressing whether or not either person is interested in or even insisting upon a prenuptial agreement. Such an agreement is essentially a contract between the two of you determining how various assets that you had prior to the marriage or that you accrued during the marriage will be divided should the marriage end in divorce. Most couples have little awareness of such a contract and have even less interest in setting one up. However, some people who own property or who have amassed considerable wealth before they get married may be interested in such a document.

Given the high rate of divorce in America, many couples are signing prenuptial agreements even before they take their wedding vows. Of course, everything that a couple says and does that is designed to facilitate a potential breakup of their marriage should be considered very carefully. Marriage is meant to be a lifetime commitment: "For better or for worse, for richer or for poorer, in sickness and in health, for as long as you both shall live." Marriage is also meant to be a relationship based upon the "one-flesh" principle by which two people have and hold everything in common.

Everything written in this book would argue against a prenuptial agreement and argue instead for an agreement to love, honor, and trust one another in all things. A marriage based upon that kind of agreement has little need for a prenuptial agreement. Nevertheless, in today's world it is a good idea to be sure this issue has at least been addressed.

Always remember that "money can't buy me love."

Let's take one more look at the lyrics of the song by the Beatles and consider it in the context of a marriage where one or both spouses are working overtime and even taking on a second job to try and get ahead financially. Every additional hour spent on the job is an hour spent away from home and away from each other. There is always a trade-off where love and money are concerned. Some couples are eager to buy and enjoy the things that more money allows them to afford, so they gladly endure any separation from each other that occurs as a result of that priority. Other couples may choose to have a little less money in order to spend a little more time with their spouse.

Where are you and your intended spouse on this question? Try to keep an open channel of communication where this balancing act is concerned. There are times when you will want to earn some extra income in order to pay for some special vacation or home renovation, or to set a little something extra aside for that college or retirement fund. On the other hand, if the desire to earn some extra income begins to place stress and strain on your marriage because you seldom, if ever, see each other, then it might be time to sing along with the Beatles, "Money can't buy me love!"

Questions to be considered

1. Are you prepared financially to get married, or will you be counting on financial support from family and friends?

2. Have you discussed whether or not you share the same financial habits as your spouse? If not, are you prepared to live with those differences? What strains might they cause in your marriage?

3. Will you make tithing a regular part of your financial planning strategy? Why or why not?

4. How does each of you feel about earning or spending money on gambling? on alcohol? on tobacco? on illegal substances?

5. How difficult will it be for both of you to live within a budget so that you are not governed by impulse buying?

6. What do you believe to be the implications of the phrase in the wedding vows that says, "for richer or for poorer?"

7. How much debt are you willing to live with? Will you seek the principle of debt-free living? Do you both know how much current debt each of you is carrying?

8. Do either of you want to draw up a prenuptial agreement? Why or why not?

7
Family
It's No Longer "Me" But "We"

THERE IS A TENDENCY for most couples to enter into marriage thinking that they aren't really a family in their right (separate from their own parents and even siblings) until they have children of their own. That isn't at all the case. As soon as you say I do, you have become a new family unit—a family of two. And, as such, you need to be prepared to navigate what psychologists would call "family dynamics."

When it comes to those family dynamics, there are two final issues to be resolved as you draw nearer to the altar and the moment when you will speak your vows. The first is what each of you believes to be the roles of husband and wife in the home and what responsibilities each of them should shoulder. The second issue involves how those roles may shift and how your entire way of life will be impacted if and when you become parents. Most couples approach marriage with many preconceived notions on these issues. Your present views on this subject are likely to be informed from one of any number of sources. We will look first at your family before children are introduced to the household.

Submit to one another out of reverence for Christ.
—Ephesians 5:21

When it comes to roles in marriage, perhaps you have observed how your parents or other older married couples divided the household responsibilities. You may have been influenced by writers or media commentators who have attempted to define what those male and female roles should be. Or, you may simply be under the impression that the Bible has some clear set of expectations regarding what roles husbands and wives should play in the home.

Les and Leslie Parrott refer to these preconceived notions as "unconscious roles."[1] The Parrotts suggest that married couples tend to follow a script, just like actors in a dramatic performance. The actors' script comes from the playwright, so in a sense they are all reading off the same page and performing in coordinated fashion. The married couple's script comes in large measure from different sets of sources— the marriages each of them witnessed while growing up, each person's idealized expectations of married life, and their personal dispositions toward performing certain roles or carrying out certain responsibilities.

Move from unconscious roles to clearly understood areas of mutual responsibility so your life together will be less stressful and more joyful.

You and your spouse may be married to each other, but most likely you are bringing two separate sets of assumptions about how you are going to live together in the context of your home and family life. If a couple is going to enjoy a long and healthy marriage, say the Parrotts, they need to "make their roles conscious."[2] Each person needs to understand quite clearly what the other person believes to be the appropriate role and responsibilities of a husband and a wife.

As a result of these unconscious roles, you may expect your spouse to be doing something within the marriage or around the house. Those expectations are based upon your own sense of unconscious roles. However, if your partner does not know what you are expecting of him or her (and vice versa)—if unconscious assumptions have not moved to both of you being "role conscious"—then unintentional non-action will inevitably result in resentments, misunderstandings, and disappointments. This can be avoided, and the best time to start sorting out these issues is before you say I do.

There is more to married life than romantic dinners and moonlit strolls.

Most couples look forward to the romance and excitement that follow their wedding day. They are thinking about dinners by candlelight and surprise gifts that serve as signs of love and affection. As important as those things are in establishing your marriage, there is more to married life than chocolate candy and "Thinking of You" notes left on the pillow or the kitchen counter. In addition to the excitement of beginning a new life together as husband and wife, there are some very mundane and practical responsibilities that have to be performed if you and your spouse are to live happily ever after.

There are meals to be prepared and a host of clean-up activities that follow every meal. There is laundry to be washed and trash to be emptied and taken for removal. There are bills to be paid on a timely basis and a house or an apartment to be regularly cleaned and maintained. Somebody will have to do the grocery shopping. Somebody will have to water the plants and flowers. Who is going to perform each of these everyday functions?

Unless assigned or assumed, some important tasks within the household may go undone all for a lack of communication.

Dozens of things need to be done on a weekly or monthly basis in order for your family life to operate smoothly. When any one of those tasks is considered separately, it may seem to be a small and insignificant matter. However, if these things are encompassed by somebody's sense of unconscious roles and they are not being performed because no time was taken "to make roles conscious," your marital bliss can come quickly to an end. Before you say I do, you need to agree on which one of you will be doing these duties, or you need to agree on how you will share in these responsibilities. You may not initially agree with each other's perception of who *should* do what around the house, but working your way through disagreements is far better than living with unconscious roles that have the effect of creating tension within your family.

I often share in counseling and in sermons this short piece of wisdom:

There was a job that needed to be done. Anybody could have done it. Everybody thought that somebody would do it, but nobody did. Nobody could understand why somebody did not do what everybody agreed could have been done by anybody. Thus, everybody was upset because somebody did not do what anybody could have done but nobody did.

Do not allow your marriage to sink into a set of unspoken expectations about nobody, somebody, anybody, and everybody. Take the time to talk about how the various roles and responsibilities associated with establishing and running a household are going to be accomplished.

Discuss roles and responsibilities with an awareness of the issues raised by feminist and womanist advocates.

Feminists and womanists seek to warn society about the abuses that have occurred because of men who have a patriarchal view of the world. Most of these men are under the impression that they are the "head of the household," and by that they mean that they are in charge of everyone and everything associated with the family. In his book *Governing the Hearth: Law and the Family in Nineteenth-Century America*, Michael Grossberg argues that assumptions about male domination have deep roots reaching back to colonial America. In 1712 one man said:

> Nothing is more gratifying to the mind of man than power or domination; and this I think myself amply possessed of, as I am the father of a family. I am perpetually taken up in giving orders, in prescribing duties, in hearing parties, in administering justice, and in distributing rewards and punishments.... In short, I look upon my family as a patriarchal sovereignty in which I am myself both priest and king.[3]

This idea of husbands and fathers who seek to dominate their family has not yet gone away. As you are preparing for marriage you and your spouse need to discuss what preconceived ideas each of you brings into the marriage.

Some women may assume that if the husband is the head of the family then he should also be the so-called breadwinner. Thus, if she has a job outside the home, she might think that her income should be for her discretionary spending. Other women may object to any notion of male headship at all or to any arrangement that implies the wife is in any way subordinate to her husband. If "male headship" characterizes how the husband understands his role, and if the wife has some concerns about that phrase and about how it will work in daily life, those concerns need to be addressed and hopefully resolved before you say I do. The wife-to-be needs to speak candidly concerning her views on this issue.

Discuss roles and responsibilities in light of the fact that more wives are now working outside of the home.

More and more women are involved in the workplace on a daily basis, and they are less and less inclined to work all day outside the home and then come home to begin another regimen of work in which the husband does not share a meaningful role. One mark of the twenty-first century may well be the number of "stay-at-home" dads who will assume most of the housekeeping and child-rearing responsibilities. A recent article in *Fortune* magazine suggests that an increasing number of men are, in fact, staying home while their wives, who hold well-paying positions in corporate America, are becoming the primary wage earners.[4] Your household may not reflect this most recent trend in American family life, but you will need to have a serious conversation concerning who is going to do what as far as performing basic household chores is concerned. Most importantly, you should have this discussion with an enlightened understanding of the responsibilities that many women carry outside the home.

The evening meal can be a great time to share responsibilities.

I have vivid memories of two meals that were served during our first year of marriage. I was a graduate student and a staff minister at a local church. My wife worked in downtown Manhattan for the federal government. One day she came home from work and began preparing dinner. I had come home earlier than she, but I relaxed in front of the evening news until dinner was placed on the table. I didn't set the table, pour the drinks, or even ask if I could do anything to help. It was early in our marriage, and I was operating with some assumptions about unconscious roles: Her role was to cook and my role was to eat.

After the meal we had a candid conversation about roles within the household. Peggy did not mind doing the cooking, especially since I was not very good at it. But, she thought it only fair that I share in some aspect of the preparation for the meal since both of us had been working that day. Not many days later, I had to attend an evening meeting at the church and would not be home to eat dinner with her. However, I put some meat and vegetables in the slow-cooker so that when Peggy got home her meal would be ready for her to enjoy. It was a small thing that took very little time on my part, but she still says it was one of the best meals she has ever had. For most of our twenty-eight years of marriage she has not worked outside the home, but I still do something at every meal to share in the preparation or in the cleanup that follows.

Marriage works best when you and your spouse share some household duties equally.

There may be specific tasks and duties that one or the other of you assumes on a regular basis. One of you may pay the bills and the other one may do most of the grocery shopping. One of you may do most of the housekeeping while the other one does most of the automobile maintenance and home repairs. However, some tasks can be shared on a regular basis. Each of you can share in doing the laundry, making up the bed, replenishing the ice tray, emptying the trash cans, washing the dishes, and replacing the toilet paper roll. Both of you can change burnt-out light bulbs and clean up after a spill in the kitchen or bathroom. If and when children become part of your family, you can take turns changing diapers, walking the floor at 2:30 A.M., and giving the baby a bath. Both of you can help with homework, serve as chauffeur to the various activities in which the child is involved, or chaperone the high-school party or the church retreat.

It is not my intent to make these decisions for you, but only to suggest that you enter your marriage with some understanding of how you will approach the roles and responsibilities that will be a part of your everyday life as husband and wife.

The biblical model for a healthy marriage is based upon partnership and not domination.

What keeps this sense of male domination alive in the context of marriage is a continued misreading or only a partial reading of the passage in Ephesians 5:21-33. Most men are familiar with the words "Wives, submit to your husbands as unto the Lord." Men are usually less familiar with the words that follow: "Husbands, love your wives, just as Christ loved the church and gave himself up for her." This passage is not designed to diminish the value or equal worth of women in any way. In a culture that was already deeply entrenched with patriarchal values, this passage tries to strike a delicate balance between the rights men were already assuming and frequently abusing and the responsibilities to their wives that the men might have been neglecting.

In saying "Wives, submit to your husbands," clearly Paul was not overturning the prevailing assumptions that ordered household relationships. Paul was urging Christian women to concede to their husbands the leadership role in the home and in the family. As old-fashioned as that may sound to some people in the feminist and womanist generation, it seems clear that Paul was not challenging the principle that in a Christian home the husband should be granted a leadership role by his wife. That role is not to be seized *from* the wife by force or intimidation; it is to be granted *by* the wife in a conscious act of entrusting that role to her husband. However, the idea of husbands as head of the household by the consent of the wife is not the part of the passage where the new revelation is found.

Paul was breaking ground when he followed the existing teachings about wives submitting to their husbands with the command that "husbands should love their wives as Christ loved the church." Paul did suggest that women should accede to the leadership of the husband. But, when the husband loves his wife as Christ loved the church, then that leadership will never result in abuse or exploitation.

This passage should not be dismissed simply because "the times have changed."

Brenda Timberlake writes about how this passage resonates to the modern era in *Gospel Today* magazine: "Even though the word *submission* is not very popular today, it's scriptural, it's Godly and it works when a husband and a wife work together."[5] Timberlake continues by linking Paul's words to husbands and wives in verses 22-25 with Paul's opening comments in verse 21, which are also overlooked or unmentioned by men who are wholeheartedly in support of wives submitting to their husbands but who express no interest in husbands loving their wives as Christ loved the church. Paul began by saying, "Submit to one another out of reverence for Christ."

Timberlake notes that "God's love is freely given, but His blessings are conditional. As you and your husband commit to submitting to one another in the fear of the Lord (Ephesians 5:21), you will begin to reap the blessings of obedience and your marriage will be blessed."[6] As you are discussing the roles and responsibilities that will help to define your family life, it is important to remember that in this much-discussed passage in Ephesians Paul was not subordinating women; he was calling for a reverence and respect for women that was unknown in the world at that time. He did that by holding men accountable in terms of how they love and cherish their wives.

Many women object to the assumption of husbands being the "head of the household." It may seem to them that such a designation serves as justification for much of the domestic violence that women have experienced at the hands of husbands who are "keeping their houses in order." Such abuse, whether physical, psychological, or emotional, would never take place if husbands loved their wives as Christ loved the church. Rather, a husband would always work in ways that are for the benefit and betterment of his wife. This view of marriage has been and, in many places across this country and around the world, continues to be revolutionary.

It is important to notice that the word Paul used when he instructed husbands to love their wives is *agapao*. This is the word that describes not only how Christ loved the church, but it also describes how God loves all of us. In a commentary on Ephesians, Francis Foulkes writes about Paul's use of *agapao* at this point by saying:

It means not only a practical concern for the welfare of the other, but a continual readiness to subordinate one's own pleasure and advantage for the benefit of the other. It implies patience and kindliness, humility and courtesy, trust and support (I Corinthians13:4-7). This love means that one is eager to understand what the needs and interests of the other are, and will do everything in his power to supply those needs and further those interests.[7]

In short, the text of Ephesians 5:21-33 does not enslave wives in a subordinate position; it releases them into a marital partnership that was unknown in the Jewish and Greco-Roman worlds at that time. Paul was not initiating an entirely new set of household codes by which Christians should be governed. Instead, he was reshaping the existing codes of that first-century culture so Christian wives would be treated with a love and respect that would not have been the case for women outside the body of Christ.

This view of Ephesians 5:22-34 is consistent with Paul's insights about the relationship between men and women in Galatians 3:28 when he declared, "There is neither Jew nor Greek, slave nor free, male nor female, for you are all one in Christ Jesus." This text reinforces the full humanity and value of women in the eyes of God and in the body of Christ. What remains is a relationship of mutual care and concern, a relationship in which the husband is granted certain leadership roles in the family but then applies that leadership in a way that blesses and benefits his wife.

Be sure to discuss whether either of your respective parents has been through a divorce.
Take time before you get married to consider whether an earlier experience of divorce has, in any way, influenced your views about marriage. My parents divorced when I was ten years old. I was hesitant to get married, in part because I did not want to replicate the marriage relationship that had most impacted my early life. When Peggy and I were contemplating marriage, I remember quoting words to her from a song by Nat King Cole that said in effect, "I'll never fall in love unless I can fall in love forever." The impact of my parents' divorce influenced my own approach to the prospects of being married myself.

It is hard to overstate how much my life was affected by the divorce of my parents, and why, to this day, the thought of a marriage ending in divorce pains me so deeply. My father left our family with significant debt that fell to my mother to pay off. We had to move out of a spacious apartment in a stable, middle-class neighborhood in Chicago. We ended up living in a dank and cramped basement apartment in a house owned by my mother's sister, who by that time had also been divorced from her husband. My mother had to work two jobs just to make ends meet, and with no father at home to oversee my growth as an adolescent, I found my friends and mentors on the streets of Chicago, and I came dangerously close to not surviving. I became a thug, a hoodlum, and a near alcoholic.

On the other hand, when Peggy and I were married in 1975, her parents had been married for nearly thirty years. She had observed her parents working through the conflicts and disagreements that arose within their home, while I had watched my parents solve their differences through a divorce. It was important for us to talk about this fundamental difference in our family backgrounds, because that difference actually influenced how receptive each of us was to the idea of getting married ourselves.

Peggy needed to know whether or not I would walk away, as my father did, when problems arose in marriage. She wanted me to know that she was willing to stay together and work out whatever problems might confront us in our marriage, just as she had seen her mother do. I am certain that the time we took to talk about this problem (which now plagues 50 percent of all couples who get married) was instrumental in our ability to remain happily married twenty-eight years after we said I do.

> *Sons are a heritage from the LORD,*
> *children a reward from him.*
> *—Psalm 127:3*

In Genesis 4 the Bible tells the story of Adam and Eve giving birth to children, Cain and Abel. In Genesis 9:1, God spoke to Noah and his sons after they came off the ark following the Flood and told them, "Be fruitful and increase in number and fill the earth." Thus, the idea of husbands and wives having and raising children was a part of God's design for creation from the beginning.

The eagerness to have children is at the heart of the biblical narrative. Abraham and Sarah, Isaac and Rebecca, and Jacob, Leah, and Rachel all wanted to have children. The lives of Samuel, John the Baptist, and Jesus all began with remarkable birth stories. The salvation plan of God played itself out through the natural cycle of parents giving birth to children. One of the truly great joys in life, and one of the most awesome responsibilities that you and your spouse may ever share, comes with the birth (or adoption) of children. The question you will want to consider is how soon after your marriage you will want to start raising a family.

You will want to discuss your individual values and strategies for child raising.

It is never too early for couples to start talking about how they would approach the task of raising their children. What kind of plans for their education must be made and when will those plans go into action? What forms of discipline will and will not be employed by both parents? What will be expected or required of children in terms of religious education and involvement in the life of the church?

Planning for a college education. You do not need to wait until your children are born to begin considering how you will pay for their education beyond high school. If you and your partner agree that a college degree is an important goal for your children to pursue, then the sooner you start your financial planning toward that goal, the better off you'll be. For some couples, their children's college and even graduate education is a mutual assumption from the beginning. Other couples, especially those who have not obtained a college degree themselves, may not place as great an emphasis on that goal. It is not for me to say what kind of education you should desire or plan for your children. I am once again suggesting an important area for consideration as you and your future spouse prepare for the possibility of parenthood.

Disciplining your children. Some parents take very seriously the old adage from Samuel Butler that says, "Spare the rod and spoil the child." That adage is doubtless based on the words of Proverbs 13:24, which advises, "He who spares the rod hates his son, but he who loves him is careful to discipline him." Some people remember the nature of parental discipline that was used upon them, and they assume the same kind of discipline should be applied when they have children of their own. Others want to pursue a very different strategy for discipline than the one they experienced in their own youth. This is a crucial topic for discussion as you and your intended spouse consider how you are going to raise your children.

Will the use of corporal punishment (e.g., spanking or hitting of any kind) be allowed? Remembering the days when my mother had made me go outside and get the switch from a nearby bush with which she would then spank me, I was determined not to repeat that practice with my own son. My wife and I talked about the issue at great length so that when the time came to discipline our son, the event would not result in a disagreement between us. I urge you to have a comparable discussion before the need for discipline actually arises.

Remember that the world has changed since you were a child. The kinds of disciplines that were normal and accepted even twenty years ago may, in today's society, result in having felony charges brought against you by police or risk involving an agency of the city or county government that is charged with safeguarding the welfare of children. Schoolteachers, coaches, and even neighbors may feel obligated to report as child abuse what you consider to be appropriate discipline.

The laws in this area have been tightened because so many children have been abused by their parents. In most cases, the parents involved never intended to be abusive; they were simply trying to discipline their children in ways that seemed appropriate to them. When you have your discussion on this issue, be sure to bear in mind that you and your spouse are not the only persons who have an interest in how you discipline your children. This issue has become a matter of deep interest and concern for our whole society because battered children show up at schools and shelters every day.

Offering religious instruction. Proverbs 22:6 says, "Train children in the way [they] should go and when [they are] old [they] will not depart from it." Parents can never accurately predict how and where their children will end up so far as religious faith is concerned. Many parents are painfully aware that they did raise their children in the way they should go, but when those children became older they departed from the faith. Nevertheless, you should discuss how you plan to introduce to and involve your children in matters of religious faith.

There are a variety of ways by which this can be done if you deem it important. As parents, you can provide religious instruction at home. You might also enroll your children in some structured form of religious education, such as your church Sunday school, an after-school Bible study group, Vacation Bible School program, or a youth group. In such settings, religious instruction can be coupled with wholesome fellowship for children who, along with their parents, share a common faith.

Many congregations have also instituted specialized "junior church" or "youth church" programs during the regular worship service. These programs tailor the religious teaching to the age and interests of the children involved. Many couples make their decision about which congregation to join based on the kinds of programs that church can offer to their children.

Be certain to discuss timing in your family planning.

Do you want to start having children right away, or do you plan to wait until your marital relationship has grown and deepened? Some couples start trying to have children right from the very beginning of their marriage, often having their first child within a year of the wedding ceremony. Other couples choose to wait for several years, preferring to enjoy life as husband and wife before they take on the additional roles of father and mother. You will want to spend some time prior to your marriage considering when and if you might want to follow the biblical admonition to "be fruitful and increase in number and fill the earth." Children are a delight and a blessing to their parents, but they also place great demands upon the home where they live.

Parenting is a full-time agenda that can and will take away from your time alone together.

From the moment they are born, children's needs have the effect of drawing time and attention away from other activities in which the

husband and wife might want to be involved. It is hard to spontane-
ously go out for an ice-cream cone, a late-night movie, or just sit together
beneath the midnight sky when a crying baby needs to be fed or changed
or simply cuddled. Peggy and I waited several years before our son was
born, and I think the time we spent nurturing our own marital relationship helped to make us better and more supportive parents.

Having said all of this, I must now observe that I have known many
couples who are numbered among my closest friends who did not wait
until later in their marriage to have children. Instead, they blended
marriage and parenthood as quickly as possible. This question of
whether or not, or when in the relationship it is most suitable to have
children is a matter of personal preference. However, you ought to at
least discuss this topic before you get married, clearly understanding
the pros and cons of whichever decision you ultimately make.

Count the costs of parenthood not only in time but in real dollars.

Raising children is not just time consuming; it is also an increasingly
expensive enterprise. There are clothes and toys to be bought, doctors'
visits and various medicines to be paid for, childcare and activity costs
to be covered, and the costs involved in transporting an infant can be
exorbitant by themselves (e.g., carriages and strollers, blankets, car
seats, diaper bags, etc.).

Needless to say, the money required to invest in child rearing is
money that is not available for you and your spouse to direct toward
events and activities that involve just the two of you. It is money that
you are not able to set aside for the eventual purchase of your own
home, for some savings plan, or for an extended vacation you may
want to take before the demands of parenthood begin. So, consider
the financial costs as well when considering when you might want to
start a family together.

If you plan to delay having children, discuss honestly and thoroughly the family planning options available to you.

If you decide you want to delay having children for some period of
time, you will also need to talk with your intended spouse about

which birth-control methods you may want to employ to achieve that end. This is not an endorsement of contraceptives, nor a suggestion that you use one or another of the available birth control options. It *is* to say that if you do not desire to have children early in your marriage, and if you are not planning to be sexually abstinent (which I do not recommend!), you will need to consider how to achieve the ends that you desire.

The first method to be considered, and one that couples used long before any of the modern contraceptives were invented, is "natural family planning." Roman Catholics who continue to resist other forms of birth control coined the expression "the rhythm method" to describe natural family planning. Such a method involves keeping track of a woman's monthly menstrual cycle in order to recognize when sexual activity is more or less likely to result in conception.

Many couples are unwilling to trust the reliability of natural family planning, and so they choose to use one or more other forms of modern birth control. These forms of contraception thrust the responsibility for preventing pregnancy on one spouse or the other. Some birth-control methods require the use of prescription products, while others involve products that are available over the counter. Some products work within the body of the woman to prevent eggs from fertilizing. Other products work to prevent male fluids from entering the woman's body in the first place. These different approaches are ultimately directed toward the same end: delaying children until later in your marital relationship. If that is your desire, then this is another discussion you will need to have before you say I do. When you do discuss this issue, be sure to consider the statistical effectiveness of and, even more importantly, the health risks associated with each of these contraceptive methods.

Please remember that adoption is another way to bring children into your home.

Having children through the process of natural childbirth is not the only way to bring children into your home and your heart. You and your intended spouse may want to consider adoption when you discuss children and family. Thousands of children need to be adopted, both across this country and around the world. It may be that you and your spouse will be unable to conceive children and that more complicated options (e.g., *in vitro* fertilization or the use of a surrogate mother) seem too daunting, expensive, or traumatic. It may be that you want to make room in your home and your hearts for children who come by birth *and* by adoption. It may be that you are getting married later in life and the idea of going through a nine-month pregnancy and the delivery of a baby is untimely or even unwise. In events such as these, adoption can be an ideal solution. Of course, the issues discussed earlier in this section remain true; you will want to consider whether to adopt children early in your marital relationship or wait a few years until your marriage and your finances have become more secure.

Not every couple has chosen to delay having children until they get married.

My comments up to this point have operated from the assumption that you will have your children after you have gotten married. That is certainly the pattern that is presumed in the Bible and the approach to family that is best for everyone involved—the children, the parents, and society as a whole. However, that is not the case in many families. I have been in the ministry for thirty years, and I know that an increasing number of couples do not wait until they are married to have children. In some couples, one or the other partner has a child from a previous relationship. Other couples express an interest in getting married only after they have had multiple children together. I recently heard a radio interview with former Representative J. C. Watts of Oklahoma. He commented that despite the fact that he is now a born-again Christian with deeply conservative social and political values, he had two children out of wedlock with the woman who eventually became his wife.

In his book, *The Hip Hop Generation: Young Blacks and the Crisis in African American Culture,* Bakari Kitwana speaks to this reality and the devastating social consequences that come with it. He mentions the phrase my "baby daddy," which is heard so frequently throughout inner-city and urban America. It refers to those instances when the father of the baby is not the husband of the mother.[8] As the pastor of a congregation located in an urban setting, this is an issue I am confronting with staggering regularity as couples who want to get married have already had one or more children together.

In mentioning this steadily increasing phenomenon, I certainly am not celebrating it or recommending this approach to others. As stated earlier, I firmly believe that it is best for everyone involved—the parents, the children, and society as a whole—if people delay having children until they are in a secure marriage in which children can be nurtured and loved. That is clearly the model affirmed throughout the Scriptures. Having acknowledged that, it would be naïve to disregard the reality that all too frequently couples are having children before the mother and father get married.

I am not suggesting that single mothers cannot raise their children alone. I have seen far too many cases where such women did an admirable job of raising children without the presence or assistance of the father of the child. But, I also know very few women in this category who did not wish for the active involvement of a husband who was the father of their offspring. My "baby daddy" is the description with which many women are left, but not necessarily the situation they desired. And, even if a woman ends up marrying her "baby daddy," it would have been preferable for the marriage to precede parenthood.

If yours will be a blended family, discuss how children from previous relationships will impact your new marriage.

It is not uncommon for a couple to get married and walk into a ready-made family with one or more children coming from a former marriage or previous relationship. In some cases, both the husband and the wife bring children that were born of previous relationships. This is what has come to be known as the *blended family.*

This type of family was given its most visible expression in the 1970s television series called *The Brady Bunch.* The show featured a middle-aged couple, each of whom brought three children from a previous marriage. On a weekly basis America became more and more conscious of the pressures and delights of the blended family. As more and more couples enter into second and even third marriages, the possibility of entering into a blended family will only increase.

Some issues must be resolved soon if you are entering into a blended family. Just because you have fallen in love with someone else does not mean your children from a former relationship are equally prepared to transfer or even share their love and allegiance with your new spouse. What will be the rules of discipline by which the children will be raised—those that prevailed in the family into which the children were born, or rules that are preferred by the new spouse? Will the children from a former marriage be expected to refer to their parent's new spouse as Mother or Father—even if they do not want to do so? If not, what will they call the new spouse— and what standards of respect and accountability will be expected? What efforts will be made to be sure that all children from former relationships feel equally included in the newly formed family? This can be especially problematic if the children of one spouse are moving into a house where children of the other spouse have been living all their lives.

In short, a second marriage may be a blessing for the adults that are involved, but if you are bringing children with you into your new relationship, you need to be sensitive to the adjustment that children from an earlier marriage are going to have to make.

* * *

I urge you and your spouse to take the time to carefully review the ideas set forth in this book before you say I do. Take the time to talk about *faith, friendship, frankness, fidelity, forgiveness, finances,* and *family.* I firmly believe it will set your relationship on a path of continued health, happiness, and long-term success!

Questions to be considered

1. What are the most important characteristics of a Christian family, and how will you incorporate those things into your marriage?

2. Have you discussed the Ephesians 5:21-33 passage, which speaks of wives submitting to their husbands and of husbands loving their wives? How will that passage influence you and your spouse?

3. What do each of you believe to be the primary roles and responsibilities of the husband and of the wife in your marriage?

4. Will both of you be working outside the home? How will that affect how you will share in work around the house?

5. Has a divorce occurred anywhere in your family history? What impact has that experience had on your view of marriage?

6. Do you both want to have children? What factors are important to each of you in considering the timing of starting a family?

7. How do you feel—both individually and as a couple—about birth control?

8. If you or your intended spouse proves to be unable to conceive, what options will you be willing to consider as a couple in pursuit of your desire for children?

9. Could you love a child from your spouse's former marriage as much as you might love the children you helped to conceive? Why or why not?

Notes

Chapter One

1. David P. Gushee. "Secret to Marriage: Spiritual Foundation." *The Plain Dealer.* (June 19, 2002), D3.
2. Ibid.
3. Alistair Begg. *Lasting Love: How to Avoid Marital Failure.* (Chicago: Moody Press, 1997), 38.
4. Ibid, 40.
5. Lee and Les Strobel. *Surviving a Spiritual Mismatch in Marriage.* (Grand Rapids, Mich.: Zondervan, 2002), 43.
6. Keith E. Whitfield, Howard J. Markman, Scott M. Stanley, and Susan L. Blumberg. *Fighting for Your African American Marriage.* (San Francisco: Jossey-Bass, 2001), 186.
7. Ibid, 187.
8. Ibid, 189.

Chapter Two

1. Neil Clark Warren, eharmony.com.
2. Keith E. Whitfield, et al., 219.
3. Ibid, 223.
4. Ibid.
5. Ibid., 224.

Chapter Four

1. Thomas and Nanette Kinkade. *The Many Loves of Marriage.* (Sisters, Ore.: Multnomah Press, 2002), 49–50.

Chapter Five

1. Les Parrott III and Leslie Parrott. *Questions Couples Ask.* (Grand Rapids, Mich.: Zondervan, 1996), 41.

2. Ibid.

3. Dietrich Bonhoeffer. *Letters and Papers from Prison.* (New York: Macmillan, 1967), 31–32.

4. Parrott, Ibid.

5. Ibid.

Chapter Six

1. Larry Burkett. *Debt-Free Living: How to Get Out of Debt and Stay Out.* (Colorado Springs: Victor Books, 1993).

2. Lonnae O'Neil Parker. "18 Months That Saved Our Marriage." *Essence.* (September 2002), 81.

3. Ibid.

Chapter Seven

1. Les Parrott III and Leslie Parrott. *Saving Your Marriage before It Starts.* (Grand Rapids, Mich.: Zondervan, 1995), 19–20.

2. Ibid, 21.

3. Michael Grossberg. *Governing the Hearth: Law and the Family in Nineteenth-Century America.* (Chapel Hill, N.C.: University of North Carolina Press, 1985), 5.

4. Betsy Morris. "Trophy Husbands." www.Fortune.com (September 27, 2002).

5. Brenda Timberlake. "Where Is the Love?" *Gospel Today.* (November/December 2002), 101.

6. Ibid, 102.

7. Francis Foulkes. *Ephesians.* (Grand Rapids, Mich.: Eerdmans, 1989), 165.

8. Bakari Kitwana. *The Hip Hop Generation: Young Blacks and the Crisis in African American Culture.* (New York: BasicCivitas Books, 2002), 115–16.

Bibliography and Other Recommended Readings

Achtemeier, Elizabeth. *Preaching about Family Relationships.* Philadelphia: Westminster Press, 1987.

Armas, Genaro C. "More Seniors Are Living Together without the Benefit of an 'I Do'." www.seatttletimes.com. July 30, 2002.

Begg, Alistair. *Lasting Love: How to Avoid Marital Failure.* Chicago: Moody Press, 1997.

Boehi, David, Brent Nelson, Jeff Schulte, and Lloyd Shadrach. *Preparing for Marriage.* Ventura, Calif.: Gospel Light Publishers, 1997.

Bonhoeffer, Dietrich. *Letters and Papers from Prison.* New York: Macmillan, 1967.

Burkett, Larry. *The Complete Financial Guide for Young Couples.* Colorado Springs: Victor Books, 1993.

———. *Debt-Free Living: How to Get Out of Debt and Stay Out.* Colorado Springs: Victor Books, 1993.

Foulkes, Francis. *Ephesians.* Grand Rapids, Mich.: Eerdmans, 1989.

Grossberg, Michael. *Governing the Hearth: Law and the Family in Nineteenth-Century America.* Chapel Hill, N.C.: The University of North Carolina Press, 1985.

Gushee, David P. "Secret to Marriage: Spiritual Foundation." *The Plain Dealer.* June 10, 2002.

Huffman, John A. *Three Ways to Help Avoid a Marriage Breakup.* www.preaching.com. December 7, 2001.

Kinkade, Thomas and Nanette Kinkade. *The Many Loves of Marriage.* Sisters, Ore.: Multnomah Publishers, 2002.

Kitwana, Bakari. *The Hip Hop Generation: Young Blacks and the Crisis in African American Culture.* New York: Basic Civitas Books, 2002.

Knight, Rich. "The Nearly Weds' Fight Club." *Leadership.* Spring 2002.

Markman, Howard J., Scott M. Stanley, and Susan L. Blumberg. *Fighting for Your Marriage.* San Francisco: Jossey-Bass, Inc., 1994.

Martens, Larry. *Life with Promise.* Hillsboro, Kans.: Kindred Press, 1982.

Mayhall, Jack and Carole Mayhall. *Marriage Takes More Than Love.* Colorado Springs: NavPress, 1978.

Melendez, Michele. "Most Say 'I Do' to Marriage, Report Says." *The Plain Dealer.* February 8, 2002.

Morris, Betsy. "Most Powerful Women in Business: Trophy Husbands." www.Fortune.com. September 27, 2002.

Parker, Lonnae O'Neal. "18 Months That Saved Our Marriage." *Essence.* September 2002.

Parrott, Les, III, and Leslie Parrott. *Questions Couples Ask: Answers to the Top 100 Marital Questions.* Grand Rapids, Mich.: Zondervan, 1996.

———. *Saving Your Marriage before It Starts.* Grand Rapids, Mich.: Zondervan, 1995.

Paul, Pamela. *The Starter Marriage and the Future of Matrimony.* New York: Random House, 2002.

Roberts, J. Deotis. *Roots of a Black Future: Family and Church.* Philadelphia: Westminster Press, 1980.

Roiphe, Anne. *Married: A Fine Predicament.* New York: Basic Books, 2002.

Small, Dwight Hervey. *Remarriage and God's Renewing Grace: A*

Positive Biblical Ethic for Divorced Christians. Grand Rapids, Mich.: Baker Books, 1986.

Smith, Wallace Charles. *The Church in the Life of the Black Family.* Valley Forge, Pa.: Judson Press, 1985.

Strobel, Lee and Leslie Strobel. *Surviving a Spiritual Mismatch.* Grand Rapids, Mich.: Zondervan, 2002.

Timberlake, Brenda. "Where Is the Love?" *Gospel Today.* Nov./Dec. 2002.

Warren, Neil Clark. eharmony.com.

Washington, Joseph R. *Marriage in Black and White.* Boston: Beacon Press, 1970.

Whitfield, Keith E., Howard J. Markman, Scott M. Stanley, and Susan L. Blumberg. *Fighting for Your African American Marriage.* San Francisco: Jossey-Bass Inc., 2001.

Wright, H. Norman and Wes Roberts. *Before You Say "I Do": A Marriage Preparation Manual for Couples.* Eugene, Ore.: Harvest House Publishers, 1977.

————. *Premarital Counseling Update.* Chicago: Moody Press, 1988.

Yancey, George and Sherelyn Whittum Yancey. *Just Don't Marry One: Interracial Dating, Marriage, and Parenting.* Valley Forge, Pa.: Judson Press, 2002.